English(Literature)　　　HS 5795

Adams

Afro-American Authors

Multi-

■ AFRO

☐ AMER

☐ ASIAN

☐ MEX

Afro-

HOUGHTON
MIFFLIN
COMPANY

BOSTON
ATLANTA
DALLAS
GENEVA, ILL.
HOPEWELL, N.J.
PALO ALTO

American Authors

William Adams

ACKNOWLEDGMENTS

Grateful acknowledgment is made to authors, publishers, and agents for their permission to reprint the following selections.

"At the Burns-Coopers'," from *Maud Martha*, by Gwendolyn Brooks. Copyright 1953 by Gwendolyn Brooks Blakely. Reprinted by permission of Harper & Row, Publishers, Inc.

"Ballad of the Landlord," from *Montage of a Dream Deferred*, by Langston Hughes. Copyright 1951 by Langston Hughes. Reprinted by permission of Harold Ober Associates, Incorporated.

"A Black Man Talks of Reaping," "The Day-breakers," and "Southern Mansion," from *Personals*, by Arna Bontemps. Copyright © 1963 by Arna Bontemps. Reprinted by permission of Harold Ober Associates, Incorporated.

"Crowns and Garlands," from *The Panther and the Lash*, by Langston Hughes. Copyright © 1967 by Arna Bontemps and George Houston Bass. Reprinted by permission of Alfred A. Knopf, Inc.

"Dark Symphony," by Melvin B. Tolson. Copyright 1944 by Dodd, Mead & Company, Inc. Reprinted by permission of Dodd, Mead & Company, Inc., from *Rendezvous with America*, by Melvin B. Tolson.

"Dream Variation" and "The Negro Speaks of Rivers," by Langston Hughes. Copyright 1926 by Alfred A. Knopf, Inc., and renewed 1954 by Langston Hughes. Reprinted from *Selected Poems*, by Langston Hughes, by permission of the publisher.

"Frederick Douglass" and "Runagate Runagate," from *Selected Poems*, by Robert Hayden. Copyright © 1966 by Robert Hayden. Reprinted by permission of October House, Inc.

From *The Life of Frederick Douglass*, published by The New American Library, Inc.

"From the Dark Tower," from *On These I Stand*, by Countee Cullen. Copyright 1927 by Harper & Row, Publishers, Inc.; renewed 1955 by Ida M. Cullen. Reprinted by permission of Harper & Row, Publishers, Inc.

"God Bless America," by John Oliver Killens. Copyright 1952 by *The California Quarterly*. Reprinted by permission of International Famous Agency.

"A Good Long Sidewalk," copyright © 1964 by William Melvin Kelley, from *Dancers on the Shore*, by William Melvin Kelley. Reprinted by permission of Doubleday & Company, Inc.

"I Have a Dream," by Martin Luther King, Jr. Copyright © 1963 by Martin Luther King, Jr. Reprinted by permission of Joan Daves.

"If We Must Die," "In Bondage," and "The White House," from *Selected Poems of Claude McKay*, copyright 1953 by Bookman Associates, Inc. Reprinted by permission of Twayne Publishers, Inc.

"Incident" and "Yet Do I Marvel," from *On These I Stand*, by Countee Cullen. Copyright 1925 by Harper & Row, Publishers, Inc.; renewed 1953 by Ida M. Cullen. Reprinted by permission of Harper & Row, Publishers, Inc.

"King of the Bingo Game," by Ralph Ellison, copyright 1944 by Ralph Ellison. Reprinted by permission of the William Morris Agency, Inc., on behalf of the author.

Library of Congress Catalog Card Number: 74-160035

ISBN: 0-395-12700-9

PHOTO CREDITS

Page 14, courtesy of Dodd, Mead & Company; p. 17, Schomberg Collection, New York; p. 20, courtesy of Harper & Row, Inc.; p. 24, Yale University Library; p. 28, courtesy of Alfred A. Knopf, Inc., photo by John Taylor; p. 46, courtesy of Harper & Row, Inc.; p. 60, courtesy of Random House, Inc.; p. 72, courtesy of Harold Ober Associates, Inc., photo by Frank O. Roberts Studio, Nashville, Tennessee; p. 76, Schomberg Collection, New York; p. 82, courtesy of Ashley Famous Agency, Inc.; p. 97, courtesy of The Dial Press, photo by Mottke Weissman; p. 108, courtesy of Doubleday & Co., Inc.; p. 115, courtesy of Junius Edwards, Inc., New York; p. 132, courtesy of October House, Inc., photo by Timothy D. Franklin; p. 137, Ebony Magazine, Johnson Publications; p. 143, Gerhard S. Gscheidle, San Francisco; p. 164, courtesy of Ronald Hobbs Literary Agency.

Contents

About the Author

WILLIAM ADAMS

 William Adams's career has included work in radio and television as well as teaching and writing. He currently is host of the television series "Right On!" while also acting as a lecturer in English, and Executive Associate Dean for Admissions and Financial Aid, for the University of Pennsylvania. He was born in Philadelphia and attended West Philadelphia High School, where he later taught English. In 1961 he was graduated from Cheyney State College, and from 1962 to 1968 he was deeply involved with Black radio in Philadelphia, working as a producer, newscaster, and disc jockey, and as host for the educational television series "Roots, Resistance, and Renaissance." During this time Mr. Adams also taught at the Lincoln University Institute and at the Institute for English Teachers. He has been an active participant in the Committee for College Placement, of which he was a founder, the Urban League, the NAACP, the Educational Equality Committee, and the National Educational Association.

Introduction

Until quite recently the Black writer in America has been a forgotten man, largely ignored, mostly unpublished or unread, and generally unknown. Only in recent years have some efforts to make him known been successful. The changing social climate in the United States, combined with efforts on the part of Black people themselves to have their contributions to the cultural life of the nation recognized, has not only made possible the rediscovery of many important Black authors and their work but has also allowed countless contemporary writers to gain access to a mass reading audience.

Black writing in America began as the Black experience in America began, in the institution of slavery. So it was not by accident that the dominant style and form of much of the earliest Black writing was the slave narrative with its overtones of active protest against an inhuman and torturous system. For Blacks in slavery, "literature" could not be an abstract art practiced for art's sake and beauty's reward. It was not a way up the social ladder of success. It was a means to fill the throbbing void that grew out of the ache and pain of the whip's lash, the chain's scar, and the endless hunger for freedom, a hunger which perhaps only enslaved men can fully feel.

To understand the Black writer and his work, one must understand the conditions under which he strove to perfect his art and at the same time transmit his message, for the message was, and in many instances continues to be, his ultimate concern. Historically it is a concern that springs from deep within himself, from that well of human emotion

1

that often finds its way only with great difficulty to the surface and into print. For those who strove to awaken the conscience of white America, fiction alone was often not enough. Only the raw material of experience hot from life itself would suffice.

A potent force operating in the life experience of the Black author was his already rich historical legacy of folklore, spirituals, gospel songs, and jazz. These elements went back to an older oral-literary heritage, some of which had managed to survive the long passage from the African continent to these strange and bewildering shores. The literary tradition brought with it an emphasis on form, style, and diction, while the oral tradition stressed communication, content, and function. Historically, for the Black writer literature was a calling not unlike the ministry, a cause within a larger cause, with freedom as the hoped-for effect.

Broadly speaking, the authors presented in this book can be said to represent three distinct traditions or modalities within the spectrum of Black writing in America. The first is the historical tradition, and it can be referred to as the mode of protest. It should be pointed out, however, that it is extremely difficult to separate any Black author ultimately from the element of protest in his work. This has been and will continue to be a main undercurrent in Black literature, simply because of necessity. As long as conditions exist which compel Black writers to speak out against racial injustice, protest will continue to be their motivating force.

The early period of protest is different from more recent traditions in that the earlier literature was addressed to a white reading public. Many of the earlier Black authors, from Phillis Wheatley to William Wells Brown, addressed the white majority with the hope that the senseless injustice and pain being inflicted upon Black people could be made known and eliminated. Obviously, in spite of Harriet Beecher Stowe and the Civil War, the essential social condition of Blacks did not improve. Subsequently, a new breed of Black writers emerged, whose principle objective was the awakening of Blacks to themselves, to their cultural heritage and values, and to their potential for breaking the social and psychological chains that bound them.

The second principal mode or tradition might be defined as the effort by the Black writer to promote a heightened awareness within the Black reading public. This mode may be called the awakening tradition. It strives to present the author's own experience as a generalization of the collective experience of Blacks in America. It attempts to awaken them to the validity of their own experience, to the contributions they have made as a group to society.

The third and final mode can be classified as the assertive tradition. It represents the Black writer's attempt to record his experiences directly, changing as little as possible, presenting his personal experiences as but a part of and not the total Black experience. He sees the whole as essentially varied and multi-faceted, organically knit together by a common historical experience and its concomitant heritage. He neither apologizes for his blackness nor celebrates it. By projecting an individual identity, however, he often reflects a collective one.

Frederick Douglass, the great abolitionist, is an excellent example of the first tradition. He had neither the time nor the inclination to think of himself as merely a literary artist. He was much too involved in the pressing business of liberating himself and those others of his race who wanted to be free. Douglass's passion was the cause of justice and the dignity of man.

His writing was largely directed toward whites in the hope that they might become more humanized by the experiences he presented to them. The excerpt from his autobiography that is included in this book attempts to reveal the growth of his own consciousness and the development of his rationale for protest against the institution of slavery.

The poet Paul Laurence Dunbar provides something of a contrast to Douglass in that he did attempt a literary style. Yet his popularity in white America was derived solely from his dialect poems which, while they might be considered masterpieces in the genre, were more expressive of the oral, nonliterary tradition. When Dunbar did attempt to move away from dialect, his poetic genius was not as readily acknowledged by his literary critics. But perhaps their objections may not have been exclusively on literary grounds, since the message of his more literary poetry is all too clear.

It is with the scholar and social scientist W. E. B. DuBois that we effectively make a transition to the second mode—from didactic protest to a conscious awakening of Black America. It is with DuBois that the role of conscious literary artist combines with that of social-activist scholar. As an advocate of the "new masses," DuBois' use of irony in the short story "On Being Crazy" (page 17) becomes a device to inform Blacks of the need to develop an awareness of themselves as people who are deserving of the full and unalienable rights of American citizenship.

Subsequently, with the advent of a growing new consciousness among the Black population, there emerged the first bona fide literary movement by Blacks in this country. This movement came to be known as the "New Negro Renaissance." Blacks became more interested in and aware of their own richly endowed heritage. There was also now a heightened awareness of the need for commitment to the ideals of social progress and group self-determination.

Not all Black authors, however, were genteel men of letters politely raising the omnipresent issue of racial injustice. Some, such as Claude McKay in "If We Must Die" (page 27), spoke out in blazing anger and voiced a cry of despair which would echo down the next several decades and beyond. If this new literary renaissance can be said to have been extensive in its array of talent, then that extensiveness was also matched by its diversity. It was a period when Black writers began to think seriously in terms of styles and forms which could be suited to their purposes. As new experiments were tried, new knowledge came to the Black writer and his public. Scholars like Alain Locke and W. E. B. DuBois, and poets like Langston Hughes and Arna Bontemps, sought new ways of expressing their cultural heritage. For Langston Hughes it was a highly successful combination of folk, jazz, and blues into a style that could reach the Black man in the street who might be unsympathetic to the more consciously literary style of an Arna Bontemps or a Melvin B. Tolson.

Among novelists, authors like Richard Wright were able to express the brutal aspects of the Black experience in a bold style that brought home the truth to Blacks who might not have been swayed by subtle literary persuasion. Wright's greatness was his ability to communicate from his own bitter experiences a realistic picture of the tortuous road down which a Black man had to travel in the America of his time. The hope of nearly every Black writer, however, remained unchanged. It was his hope that his own work would be an instrument for change in the struggle for justice and equality.

Of all contemporary Black authors, perhaps the novelist Ralph Ellison stands alone, somewhat aloof, in his refusal to be reduced to a common denominator and thereby defined only as a Black writer. Certainly as controversial as he is talented, Ellison sees the Black man in America as the product of a fusion of many diverse cultures, with the African heritage providing the base. His own literary emphasis, however, can be said to exemplify the awareness modality. In his masterful prize-winning novel *Invisible Man* his protest against the dehumanized existence of his Black protagonist was in fact subordinate to his principle theme, which stressed the dehumanizing aspects of industrialized man and society. He attempted to get readers both Black and white to see the Black man in America for what he truly is—an integral part of the whole amalgam of the American national character.

The third and final mode, the assertive tradition, represents the writings of many contemporary Black authors. Characteristic of this mode is the attempt to present the Black experience "like it is," without embellishment or adornment. Focus is upon experiences which have roots in a subculture nurtured on poverty and alienation. The goal of many contemporary Black writers is to present the reader with a self-view that is both honest and positive.

While the mode itself is relatively uniform in its assertion, there is, however, a broad range of approaches and attitudes on the part of individual authors. James Baldwin, felt by many critics to be one of the finest prose stylists writing today, is concerned almost exclusively with problems of racial conflict as they relate to individual identities. More than most contemporary Black authors, he reveals a struggle to settle the conflicts within himself as well as those arising from the society-at-large out of which he as an artist strives to shape his destiny both as a writer and as a man.

By contrast, a writer like William Melvin Kelley has something different to say about the world in which he as a Black writer lives and writes. In Kelley the agony of being Black in America is seen less against the background of an omniscient white society. It is ultimately a more subtle, deeply human agony issuing from the human condition.

Imamu Amiri Baraka (LeRoi Jones) is perhaps the Black writer among his contemporary peers who creatively, so to speak, has traveled the greatest distance. His early career as a writer reflected much of the avant-garde preoccupation with revolutionary literary style and form which was characteristic of the "beat generation" movement in the 1950s. As the "beat movement" dissolved, however, he continued to mature as a writer, and his political and social consciousness began to find a deeper expression in the Black literary renaissance of the 1960s.

Eldridge Cleaver represents yet another type of literary figure among present-day Black writers. He clearly can be seen as expressive of the assertive modality, yet since strong elements of protest are central to his work, he is a writer whose literary efforts are adjunct to his work as a political social polemicist.

Although there is considerably more distance to be traveled along the road of social progress, the indelible imprint the Black writer has made upon the body of American culture can no longer be ignored. His contribution is now being recognized for what it is, a vital part of the form and substance of nearly all that is natively American.

Frederick Douglass

1817–1895

Born a slave in Talbot County, Maryland, Frederick Douglass became a house servant at the age of eight and began to learn reading and writing from his master's wife. In 1838 he escaped from slavery and fled to New York disguised as a sailor. Douglass was an active leader in the antislavery movement in America, and after the Civil War he was an ardent worker for civil rights. Author of several "slave narratives," Douglass wrote three autobiographies, of which Narrative of the Life of Frederick Douglass, an American Slave *is best known. Douglass acted as President Lincoln's adviser in determining the role of the Black man in the Civil War. During Reconstruction he held many official positions in government and eventually became Minister to Haiti.*

FROM
The Life of Frederick Douglass

I lived in Master Hugh's family about seven years. During this time, I succeeded in learning to read and write. In accomplishing this, I was compelled to resort to various stratagems. I had no regular teacher. My mistress, who had kindly commenced to instruct me, had, in compliance with

7

the advice and direction of her husband, not only ceased to instruct, but had set her face against my being instructed by anyone else. It is due, however, to my mistress to say of her that she did not adopt this course of treatment immediately. She at first lacked the depravity indispensable to shutting me up in mental darkness. It was at least necessary for her to have some training in the exercise of irresponsible power, to make her equal to the task of treating me as though I were a brute.

My mistress was, as I have said, a kind and tender-hearted woman; and in the simplicity of her soul she commenced, when I first went to live with her, to treat me as she supposed one human being ought to treat another. In entering upon the duties of a slaveholder, she did not seem to perceive that I sustained to her the relation of a mere chattel,[1] and that for her to treat me as a human being was not only wrong, but dangerously so. Slavery proved as injurious to her as it did to me. When I went there, she was a pious, warm, and tenderhearted woman. There was no sorrow or suffering for which she had not a tear. She had bread for the hungry, clothes for the naked, and comfort for every mourner that came within her reach. Slavery soon proved its ability to divest her of these heavenly qualities. Under its influence, the tender heart became stone, and the lamblike disposition gave way to one of tigerlike fierceness. The first step in her downward course was in her ceasing to instruct me. She now commenced to practice her husband's precepts. She finally became even more violent in her opposition than her husband himself. She was not satisfied with simply doing as well as he had commanded; she seemed anxious to do better. Nothing seemed to make her more angry than to see me with a newspaper. She seemed to think that here lay the danger. I have had her rush at me with a face made all up of fury, and snatch from me a newspaper, in a manner that fully revealed her apprehension. She was an apt woman; and a little experience soon demonstrated, to her satisfaction, that education and slavery were incompatible with each other.

[1] CHATTEL: item of property.

From this time I was most narrowly watched. If I was in a separate room any considerable length of time, I was sure to be suspected of having a book, and was at once called to give an account of myself. All this, however, was too late. The first step had been taken. Mistress, in teaching me the alphabet, had given me the *inch*, and no precaution could prevent me from taking the *ell*.

The plan which I adopted, and the one by which I was most successful, was that of making friends of all the little white boys whom I met in the street. As many of these as I could, I converted into teachers. With their kindly aid, obtained at different times and in different places, I finally succeeded in learning to read. When I was sent on errands, I always took my book with me, and by doing one part of my errand quickly, I found time to get a lesson before my return. I used also to carry bread with me, enough of which was always in the house, and to which I was always welcome; for I was much better off in this regard than many of the poor white children in our neighborhood. This bread I used to bestow upon the hungry little urchins, who, in return, would give me that more valuable bread of knowledge. I am strongly tempted to give the names of two or three of those little boys, as a testimonial of the gratitude and affection I bear them; but prudence forbids—not that it would injure me, but it might embarrass them; for it is almost an unpardonable offense to teach slaves to read in this Christian country. It is enough to say of the dear little fellows that they lived on Philpot Street, very near Durgin and Bailey's shipyard. I used to talk this matter of slavery over with them. I would sometimes say to them I wished I could be as free as they would be when they got to be men. "You will be free as soon as you are twenty-one, *but I am a slave for life!* Have not I as good a right to be free as you have?" These words used to trouble them; they would express for me the liveliest sympathy, and console me with the hope that something would occur by which I might be free.

I was now about twelve years old, and the thought of being *a slave for life* began to bear heavily upon my heart. Just about this time, I got hold of a book entitled *The*

Columbian Orator. Every opportunity I got, I used to read this book. Among much of other interesting matter, I found in it a dialogue between a master and his slave. The slave was represented as having run away from his master three times. The dialogue represented the conversation which took place between them when the slave was retaken the third time. In this dialogue, the whole argument in behalf of slavery was brought forward by the master, all of which was disposed of by the slave. The slave was made to say some very smart as well as impressive things in reply to his master—things which had the desired though unexpected effect; for the conversation resulted in the voluntary emancipation of the slave on the part of the master.

In the same book, I met with one of Sheridan's mighty speeches on and in behalf of Catholic emancipation. These were choice documents to me. I read them over and over again with unabated interest. They gave tongue to interesting thoughts of my own soul, which had frequently flashed through my mind and died away for want of utterance. The moral which I gained from the dialogue was the power of truth over the conscience of even a slaveholder. What I got from Sheridan was a bold denunciation of slavery, and a powerful vindication of human rights. The reading of these documents enabled me to utter my thoughts, and to meet the arguments brought forward to sustain slavery; but while they relieved me of one difficulty, they brought on another even more painful than the one of which I was relieved. The more I read, the more I was led to abhor and detest my enslavers. I could regard them in no other light than a band of successful robbers, who had left their homes, and gone to Africa, and stolen us from our homes, and in a strange land reduced us to slavery. I loathed them as being the meanest as well as the most wicked of men. As I read and contemplated the subject, behold! that very discontentment which Master Hugh had predicted would follow my learning to read had already come, to torment and sting my soul to unutterable anguish. As I writhed under it, I would at times feel that learning to read had been a curse rather than a blessing. It had given me a view of my

wretched condition, without the remedy. It opened my
eyes to the horrible pit, but to no ladder upon which to
get out. In moments of agony, I envied my fellow slaves for
their stupidity. I have often wished myself a beast. I pre-
ferred the condition of the meanest reptile to my own. Anything, no matter what, to get rid of thinking! It was this
everlasting thinking of my condition that tormented me.
There was no getting rid of it. It was pressed upon me by
every object within sight or hearing, animate or inanimate.
The silver trump of freedom had roused my soul to eternal
wakefulness. Freedom now appeared, to disappear no more
forever. It was heard in every sound, and seen in every
thing. It was ever present to torment me with a sense of
my wretched condition. I saw nothing without seeing it, I
heard nothing without hearing it, and felt nothing without
feeling it. It looked from every star, it smiled in every calm,
breathed in every wind, and moved in every storm.

I often found myself regretting my own existence, and
wishing myself dead; and but for the hope of being free, I
have no doubt but that I should have killed myself, or done
something for which I should have been killed. While in
this state of mind, I was eager to hear anyone speak of
slavery. I was a ready listener. Every little while, I could
hear something about the abolitionists. It was some time
before I found what the word meant. It was always used in
such connections as to make it an interesting word to me.
If a slave ran away and succeeded in getting clear, or if a
slave killed his master, set fire to a barn, or did any thing
very wrong in the mind of a slaveholder, it was spoken of as
the fruit of *abolition*. Hearing the word in this connection
very often, I set about learning what it meant. The diction-
ary afforded me little or no help. I found it was "the act of
abolishing," but then I did not know what was to be abol-
ished. Here I was perplexed. I did not dare to ask anyone
about its meaning, for I was satisfied that it was something
they wanted me to know very little about. After a patient
waiting, I got one of our city papers, containing an account
of the number of petitions from the North, praying for the
abolition of slavery in the District of Columbia, and of the

slave trade between the states. From this time I understood the words *abolition* and *abolitionist,* and always drew near when that word was spoken, expecting to hear something of importance to myself and fellow slaves. The light broke in upon me by degrees. I went one day down on the wharf of Mr. Waters, and seeing two Irishmen unloading a scow of stone, I went, unasked, and helped them. When we had finished, one of them came to me and asked me if I were a slave. I told him I was. He asked, "Are ye a slave for life?" I told him that I was. The good Irishman seemed to be deeply affected by the statement. He said to the other that it was a pity so fine a little fellow as myself should be a slave for life. He said it was a shame to hold me. They both advised me to run away to the North; that I should find friends there, and that I should be free. I pretended not to be interested in what they said and treated them as if I did not understand them, for I feared they might be treacherous. White men have been known to encourage slaves to escape, and then, to get the reward, catch them and return them to their masters. I was afraid that these seemingly good men might use me so; but nevertheless remembered their advice, and from that time I resolved to run away. I looked forward to a time at which it would be safe for me to escape. I was too young to think of doing so immediately; besides, I wished to learn how to write, as I might have occasion to write my own pass. I consoled myself with the hope that I should one day find a good chance. Meanwhile, I would learn to write.

The idea as to how I might learn to write was suggested to me by being in Durgin and Bailey's shipyard, and frequently seeing the ship carpenters, after hewing and getting a piece of timber ready for use, write on the timber the name of that part of the ship for which it was intended. When a piece of timber was intended for the larboard side, it would be marked thus—"L." When a piece was for the starboard side, it would be marked thus—"S." A piece for the larboard side forward would be marked thus—"L. F." When a piece was for starboard side forward, it would be marked thus—"S.F." For larboard aft, it would be marked thus—"L. A." For starboard aft, it would be marked thus— "S. A." I soon learned the names of these letters, and for what they were intended when placed upon a piece of timber in the shipyard. I immediately commenced copying them, and in a short time was able to make the four letters named. After that, when I met with any boy who I knew could write, I would tell him I could write as well as he. The next word would be, "I don't believe you. Let me see you try it." I would then make the letters which I had been so fortunate as to learn, and ask him to beat that. In this way I got a good many lessons in writing, which it is quite possible I should never have gotten in any other way. During this time, my copybook was the board fence, brick wall, and pavement; my pen and ink was a lump of chalk. With these, I learned mainly how to write. I then commenced and continued copying the italics in *Webster's Spelling Book* until I could make them all without looking on the book. By this time, my little Master Thomas had gone to school and learned how to write, and had written over a number of copybooks. These had been brought home, and shown to some of our near neighbors, and then laid aside. My mistress used to go to class meeting at the Wilk Street meetinghouse every Monday afternoon and leave me to take care of the house. When left thus, I used to spend the time in writing in the spaces left in Master Thomas's copybook, copying what he had written. I continued to do this until I could write a hand very similar to that of Master Thomas. Thus, after a long, tedious effort for years, I finally succeeded in learning how to write.

FOR DISCUSSION

1. In this selection, Douglass describes how owning a slave has a degrading effect on his mistress's character. Do you think that owning a slave would generally have such an effect? Why?

2. Douglass says it was "not only wrong, but dangerously so" to treat a slave like a human being. What does he mean?

Paul Laurence Dunbar

1872–1906

The first Black poet to receive general acclaim in America, Paul Laurence Dunbar was the son of former slaves. As a student, he maintained an excellent academic record, but social prejudice barred him from pursuing a journalistic career. He privately published his first book of poetry while working as an elevator operator in a Dayton, Ohio, hotel. The publication of his second volume of poetry attracted the attention of William Dean Howells, an influential critic who became Dunbar's enthusiastic patron. Dunbar died at thirty-four, a victim of tuberculosis. In his brief career, he produced four novels, four collections of short stories, and more than four hundred poems, plays, song lyrics, essays, and articles.

We Wear the Mask

We wear the mask that grins and lies,
It hides our cheeks and shades our eyes—
This debt we pay to human guile;
With torn and bleeding hearts we smile,
And mouth with myriad subtleties.

Why should the world be over-wise,
In counting all our tears and sighs?

Nay, let them only see us, while
  We wear the mask.

We smile, but O great Christ, our cries
To thee from tortured souls arise.
We sing, but oh the clay is vile
Beneath our feet, and long the mile;
But let the world dream otherwise,
  We wear the mask!

FOR DISCUSSION

What is the "mask"? What does it conceal?

Sympathy

I know what the caged bird feels, alas!
When the sun is bright on the upland slopes;
When the wind stirs soft through the springing grass,
And the river flows like a stream of glass;
When the first bird sings and the first bud opes,
And the faint perfume from its chalice steals—
I know what the caged bird feels!

I know why the caged bird beats his wing
Till its blood is red on the cruel bars;
For he must fly back to his perch and cling
When he fain would be on the bough a-swing;
And a pain still throbs in the old, old scars
And they pulse again with a keener sting—
I know why he beats his wing!

I know why the caged bird sings, ah me,
When his wing is bruised and his bosom sore—
When he beats his bars and he would be free;
It is not a carol of joy or glee,
But a prayer that he sends from his heart's deep core,
But a plea, that upward to heaven he flings—
I know why the caged bird sings!

FOR DISCUSSION

Why does the poet feel sympathy for the bird? What is the poet's
response to his own condition?

W. E. B. DuBois

1868–1963

An ardent civil rights worker, author, editor, and scholar, W. E. B. DuBois believed that "the problem of the Twentieth Century is the problem of the color line." During his long lifetime, he championed human rights. DuBois was educated at Fisk, Harvard, and the University of Berlin; he taught history and economics in several universities, including Atlanta University. When he retired from teaching, DuBois helped to set up and direct the NAACP. He founded, edited, and published The Crisis, *the NAACP magazine. He wrote numerous books on Africa and edited the* Encyclopedia Africana *while living in Africa. He also wrote articles, historical and sociological books, poems, autobiography, and novels. Among the best-known of his works are* The Souls of Black Folk, Black Reconstruction, *and* Dusk at Dawn. *DuBois died in Ghana at the age of ninety-five.*

On Being Crazy

It was one o'clock and I was hungry. I walked into a restaurant, seated myself, and reached for the bill of fare. My table companion rose.

"Sir," said he, "do you wish to force your company on those who do not want you?"

No, said I, I wish to eat.

17

"Are you aware, sir, that this is social equality?"

Nothing of the sort, sir, it is hunger—and I ate.

The day's work done, I sought the theater. As I sank into my seat, the lady shrank and squirmed.

I beg pardon, I said.

"Do you enjoy being where you are not wanted?" she asked coldly.

Oh no, I said.

"Well, you are not wanted here."

I was surprised. I fear you are mistaken, I said; I certainly want the music, and I like to think the music wants me to listen to it.

"Usher," said the lady, "this is social equality."

"No, madam," said the usher, "it is the second movement of Beethoven's Fifth Symphony."

After the theater, I sought the hotel where I had sent my baggage. The clerk scowled.

"What do you want?"

Rest, I said.

"This is a white hotel," he said.

I looked around. Such a color scheme requires a great deal of cleaning, I said, but I don't know that I object.

"We object," said he.

Then why, I began, but he interrupted.

"We don't keep niggers," he said; "we don't want social equality."

Neither do I, I replied gently; I want a bed.

I walked thoughtfully to the train. I'll take a sleeper through Texas. I'm a little bit dissatisfied with this town.

"Can't sell you one."

I only want to hire it, said I, for a couple of nights.

"Can't sell you a sleeper in Texas," he maintained. "They consider that social equality."

I consider it barbarism, I said, and I think I'll walk.

Walking, I met another wayfarer, who immediately walked to the other side of the road, where it was muddy. I asked his reason.

"Niggers is dirty," he said.

So is mud, said I. Moreover, I am not as dirty as you—yet.

"But you're a nigger, ain't you?" he asked.

My grandfather was so called.

"Well then!" he answered triumphantly.

Do you live in the South? I persisted, pleasantly.

"Sure," he growled, "and starve there."

I should think you and the Negroes should get together and vote out starvation.

"We don't let them vote."

We? Why not? I said in surprise.

"Niggers is too ignorant to vote."

But, I said, I am not so ignorant as you.

"But you're a nigger."

Yes, I'm certainly what you mean by that.

"Well then!" he returned, with that curiously inconsequential note of triumph. "Moreover," he said, "I don't want my sister to marry a nigger."

I had not seen his sister, so I merely murmured, let her say no.

"By God, you shan't marry her, even if she said yes."

But—but I don't want to marry her, I answered, a little perturbed at the personal turn.

"Why not!" he yelled, angrier than ever.

Because I'm already married and I rather like my wife.

"Is she a nigger?" he asked suspiciously.

Well, I said again, her grandmother was called that.

"Well then!" he shouted in that oddly illogical way.

I gave up.

Go on, I said, either you are crazy or I am.

"We both are," he said as he trotted along in the mud.

FOR DISCUSSION

1. Why is this story called "On Being Crazy"? At the end, the Black man says to the white man walking opposite him, "Either you are crazy or I am." What does the white man mean when he replies, "We both are"?

2. What makes this story ironic? What mood is created by the Black man's attitude or tone? The white man sees himself as very different from the Black man. What are these differences? Why do they seem humorous?

Countee Cullen

1903–1946

Born in New York City and "reared in the conservative atmosphere of a Methodist parsonage," Countee Cullen became a central figure in the Harlem Renaissance, a period of artistic achievement by Black writers which occurred during the 1920s. Elected to Phi Beta Kappa, he was graduated from New York University and received his M.A. from Harvard before returning to New York to teach in the Harlem public schools. He became assistant editor of Opportunity, *a magazine which published many of the writers of the Harlem Renaissance, and also edited* Caroling Dusk, *an anthology of verse by Black poets. A classicist in his choice of poetic forms, Cullen published his first volume of poetry while still an undergraduate. His poems have been collected in the volume* On These I Stand.

Incident

Once riding in old Baltimore,
Heart-filled, head-filled with glee,
I saw a Baltimorean
Keep looking straight at me.

Now I was eight and very small,
And he was no whit bigger,

20

And so I smiled, but he poked out
His tongue, and called me "Nigger."

I saw the whole of Baltimore
From May until December;
Of all the things that happened there
That's all that I remember.

FOR DISCUSSION

Why is this "incident" the only thing that the speaker remembers
from his seven months in Baltimore?

Yet Do I Marvel

I doubt not God is good, well-meaning, kind,
And did He stoop to quibble could tell why
The little buried mole continues blind,
Why flesh that mirrors Him must some day die,
Makes plain the reason tortured Tantalus[1]
Is baited by the fickle fruit, declare
If merely brute caprice dooms Sisyphus[2]
To struggle up a never-ending stair.
Inscrutable His ways are, and immune
To catechism by a mind too strewn
With petty cares to slightly understand
What awful brain compels His awful hand.
Yet do I marvel at this curious thing:
To make a poet black, and bid him sing!

[1] TANTALUS (tăn′tə·ləs): In Greek mythology, this son of Zeus was tormented (tantalized) in Hades by being prevented from reaching the fruit and water he craved.
[2] SISYPHUS (sĭs′ĭ·fəs): legendary Greek king condemned, after death, to unendingly repeat the rolling of a heavy stone up a hill.

FOR DISCUSSION

The poem deals with the traditional question of why God has created a world containing evil. What is the poet's answer to this question? What is the meaning of the closing couplet?

From the Dark Tower

We shall not always plant while others reap
The golden increment[1] of bursting fruit,
Not always countenance, abject and mute,
That lesser men should hold their brothers cheap;
Not everlastingly while others sleep
Shall we beguile their limbs with mellow flute,
Not always bend to some more subtle brute;
We were not made eternally to weep.

The night whose sable breast relieves the stark
White stars is no less lovely, being dark;
And there are buds that cannot bloom at all
In light, but crumple, piteous, and fall;
So in the dark we hide the heart that bleeds,
And wait, and tend our agonizing seeds.

[1] INCREMENT (ĭn′krə·mənt): gain; increase.

FOR DISCUSSION

1. Countee Cullen uses images of light and darkness and images of planting and harvesting. Find all the instances of both kinds of imagery. How are the two kinds of imagery related?

2. How do the rhymes in the first stanza underscore the contrast between the Black man and his oppressor? What ideas does Countee Cullen express in each stanza? How are the two stanzas related?

Claude McKay

1891–1948

One of eleven children, Claude McKay was the son of a Jamaican farmer. McKay, whose first book of poetry, Songs of Jamaica, *was written in dialect, became the first Black man awarded the medal of the Institute of Arts and Sciences in Jamaica in 1912, before he left the West Indies to attend Tuskegee Institute. He left Tuskegee after three months, but he continued his education at Kansas State University before going to New York to write. Supporting himself by a variety of menial jobs, he was prominent in the Harlem Renaissance and in the American radical press of the 1920s. He moved between the United States and Europe in the years that followed, distinguishing himself as a novelist, short-story writer, and poet. Illness marked his later years, and he died in poverty.*

In Bondage

I would be wandering in distant fields
Where man, and bird, and beast, lives leisurely,
And the old earth is kind, and ever yields
Her goodly gifts to all her children free;
Where life is fairer, lighter, less demanding,
And boys and girls have time and space for play

24

Before they come to years of understanding—
Somewhere I would be singing, far away.
For life is greater than the thousand wars
Men wage for it in their insatiate lust,
And will remain like the eternal stars,
When all that shines today is drift and dust
But I am bound with you in your mean graves,
O black men, simple slaves of ruthless slaves.

FOR DISCUSSION

1. What kind of world is the speaker describing in lines 1–8? How is the world described in lines 9–12 different?

2. What does "life" in line 9 mean?

3. Who are the "simple slaves" and "ruthless slaves" in line 14? Why is the speaker unable to achieve the dream expressed in line 8?

The White House

Your door is shut against my tightened face,
And I am sharp as steel with discontent;
But I possess the courage and the grace
To bear my anger proudly and unbent.
The pavement slabs burn loose beneath my feet,
A chafing savage, down the decent street;
And passion rends my vitals as I pass,
Where boldly shines your shuttered door of glass.
Oh I must search for wisdom every hour,
Deep in my wrathful bosom sore and raw,
And find in it the superhuman power
To hold me to the letter of your law!
Oh I must keep my heart inviolate
Against the potent poison of your hate.

FOR DISCUSSION

1. What does the white house symbolize?

2. Describe the feelings of the speaker. What does he mean by keeping his "heart inviolate/Against the potent poison of your hate"?

If We Must Die

If we must die—let it not be like hogs
Hunted and penned in an inglorious spot,
While round us bark the mad and hungry dogs,
Making their mock at our accursed lot.
If we must die—oh, let us nobly die,
So that our precious blood may not be shed
In vain; then even the monsters we defy
Shall be constrained to honor us though dead!
Oh, Kinsmen! We must meet the common foe;
Though far outnumbered, let us show us brave,
And for their thousand blows deal one deathblow!
What though before us lies the open grave?
Like men we'll face the murderous, cowardly pack,
Pressed to the wall, dying, but fighting back!

FOR DISCUSSION

Animal imagery is important to the meaning of this poem. Find
the instances of this imagery and then explain what it suggests.
How do the "men . . . fighting back" in the concluding lines contrast with the hogs in the opening lines?

Langston Hughes

1902–1967

*In describing himself Langston Hughes observed, "I like:
Tristan, goat's milk, short novels, lyric poems, heat, simple
folk, boats, and bullfights; I dislike Aïda, parsnips, long
novels, narrative poems, cold, pretentious folk, busses, and
bridge." Author of more than thirty books, Hughes traveled
widely, working as a seaman on voyages to Europe and
Africa. At various times he lived in Mexico, Paris, Italy,
Spain, and Russia. He wrote a newspaper column for the*
Chicago Defender *in which he created Jesse B. Simple, a
Harlem character who was featured in several short-story
collections as well as in the author's stage musical* Simply
Heavenly. *Called the "original jazz poet" by Arna Bontemps, Hughes wrote verse which reflects the tempo and
mood of jazz. He also distinguished himself as a writer of
short stories, plays, novels, movie scripts, and songs.*

Dream Variation

To fling my arms wide
In some place of the sun,
To whirl and to dance
Till the white day is done.
Then rest at cool evening

28

Beneath a tall tree
While night comes on gently,
    Dark like me—
That is my dream!

To fling my arms wide
In the face of the sun,
Dance! Whirl! Whirl!
Till the quick day is done.
Rest at pale evening . . .
A tall, slim tree . . .
Night coming tenderly
    Black like me.

FOR DISCUSSION

1. What is the significance of the speaker's dream?

2. What is the significance of the title?

The Negro Speaks of Rivers

I've known rivers:
I've known rivers ancient as the world and older than the
    flow of human blood in human veins.

My soul has grown deep like the rivers.

I bathed in the Euphrates when dawns were young.
I built my hut near the Congo and it lulled me to sleep.
I looked upon the Nile and raised the pyramids above it.
I heard the singing of the Mississippi when Abe Lincoln
    went down to New Orleans, and I've seen its muddy
    bosom turn all golden in the sunset.

I've known rivers:
Ancient, dusky rivers.

My soul has grown deep like the rivers.

FOR DISCUSSION

What do rivers stand for in this poem? What is the effect of the
repetition of the word *rivers?*

On the Road

He was not interested in the snow. When he got off the freight, one early evening during the depression, Sargeant never even noticed the snow. But he must have felt it seeping down his neck, cold, wet, sopping in his shoes. But if you had asked him, he wouldn't have known it was snowing. Sargeant didn't see the snow, not even under the bright lights of the main street, falling white and flaky against the night. He was too hungry, too sleepy, too tired.

The Reverend Mr. Dorset, however, saw the snow when he switched on his porch light, opened the front door of his parsonage, and found standing there before him a big black man with snow on his face, a human piece of night with snow on his face—obviously unemployed.

Said the Reverend Mr. Dorset before Sargeant even realized he'd opened his mouth: "I'm sorry. No! Go right on down this street four blocks and turn to your left, walk up seven, and you'll see the Relief Shelter. I'm sorry. No!" He shut the door.

Sargeant wanted to tell the holy man that he had already been to the Relief Shelter, been to hundreds of relief shelters during the depression years; the beds were always gone, and supper was over; the place was full, and they drew the color line anyhow. But the minister said, "No," and shut the door. Evidently he didn't want to hear about it. And he *had* a door to shut.

The big black man turned away. And even yet he didn't see the snow, walking right into it. Maybe he sensed it, cold, wet, sticking to his jaws, wet on his black hands, sopping in his shoes. He stopped and stood on the sidewalk hunched over—hungry, sleepy, cold—looking up and down. Then he looked right where he was—in front of a church. Of course! A church! Sure, right next to a parsonage, certainly a church.

It had *two* doors.

31

Broad white steps in the night all snowy white. Two high arched doors with slender stone pillars on either side. And way up, a round lacy window with a stone crucifix in the middle and Christ on the crucifix in stone. All this was pale in the street lights, solid and stony pale in the snow.

Sargeant blinked. When he looked up, the snow fell into his eyes. For the first time that night he *saw* the snow. He shook his head. He shook the snow from his coat sleeves, felt hungry, felt lost, felt not lost, felt cold. He walked up the steps of the church. He knocked at the door. No answer. He tried the handle. Locked. He put his shoulder against the door, and his long black body slanted like a ramrod. He pushed. With loud rhythmic grunts, like the grunts in a chain-gang song, he pushed against the door.

"I'm tired . . . Huh! . . . Hongry . . . Uh! . . . I'm sleepy . . . Huh! I'm cold . . . I got to sleep somewheres," Sargeant said. "This here is a church, ain't it? Well, uh!"

He pushed against the door.

Suddenly, with an undue cracking and screaking, the door began to give way to the tall black Negro who pushed ferociously against it.

By now two or three white people had stopped in the street, and Sargeant was vaguely aware of some of them yelling at him concerning the door. Three or four more came running, yelling at him.

"Hey!" they said. "Hey!"

"Uh-huh," answered the big tall Negro, "I know it's a white folks' church, but I got to sleep somewhere." He gave another lunge at the door. "Huh!"

And the door broke open.

But just when the door gave way, two white cops arrived in a car, ran up the steps with their clubs, and grabbed Sargeant. But Sargeant for once had no intention of being pulled or pushed away from the door.

Sargeant grabbed, but not for anything so weak as a broken door. He grabbed for one of the tall stone pillars beside the door, grabbed at it and caught it. And held it. The cops pulled and Sargeant pulled. Most of the people in the street got behind the cops and helped them pull.

"A big black unemployed Negro holding on to our church!" thought the people. "The idea!"

The cops began to beat Sargeant over the head, and nobody protested. But he held on.

And then the church fell down.

Gradually, the big stone front of the church fell down, the walls and the rafters, the crucifix and the Christ. Then the whole thing fell down, covering the cops and the people with bricks and stones and debris. The whole church fell down in the snow.

Sargeant got out from under the church and went walking on up the street with the stone pillar on his shoulder. He was under the impression that he had buried the parsonage and the Reverend Mr. Dorset who said, "No!" So he laughed and threw the pillar six blocks up the street and went on.

Sargeant thought he was alone, but listening to the *crunch, crunch, crunch* on the snow of his own footsteps, he heard other footsteps, too, doubling his own. He looked around, and there was Christ walking along beside him, the same Christ that had been on the cross on the church—still stone with a rough stone surface, walking along beside him just like he was broken off the cross when the church fell down.

"Well, I'll be dogged," said Sargeant. "This here's the first time I ever seed you off the cross."

"Yes," said Christ, crunching his feet in the snow. "You had to pull the church down to get me off the cross."

"You glad?" said Sargeant.

"I sure am," said Christ.

They both laughed.

"I'm a hell of a fellow, ain't I?" said Sargeant. "Done pulled the church down!"

"You did a good job," said Christ. "They have kept me nailed on a cross for nearly two thousand years."

"Whee-ee-e!" said Sargeant. "I know you are glad to get off."

"I sure am," said Christ.

They walked on in the snow. Sargeant looked at the man of stone.

"And you have been up there two thousand years?"

"I sure have," Christ said.

"Well, if I had a little cash," said Sargeant, "I'd show you around a bit."

"I been around," said Christ.

"Yeah, but that was a long time ago."

"All the same," said Christ, "I've been around."

They walked on in the snow until they came to the railroad yards. Sargeant was tired, sweating and tired.

"Where you goin'?" Sargeant said, stopping by the tracks. He looked at Christ. Sargeant said, "I'm just a bum on the road. How about you? Where you goin'?"

"God knows," Christ said, "but I'm leavin' here."

They saw the red and green lights of the railroad yard half veiled by the snow that fell out of the night. Away down the track they saw a fire in a hobo jungle.

"I can go there and sleep," Sargeant said.

"You can?"

"Sure," said Sargeant. "That place ain't got no doors."

Outside the town, along the tracks, there were barren trees and bushes below the embankment, snow-gray in the dark. And down among the trees and bushes there were makeshift houses made out of boxes and tin and old pieces of wood and canvas. You couldn't see them in the dark, but you knew they were there if you'd ever been on the road, if you had ever lived with the homeless and hungry in a depression.

"I'm side-tracking," Sargeant said. "I'm tired."

"I'm gonna make it on to Kansas City," said Christ.

"O.K.," Sargeant said. "So long!"

He went down into the hobo jungle and found himself a place to sleep. He never did see Christ no more. About 6:00 A.M. a freight came by. Sargeant scrambled out of the jungle with a dozen or so more hobos and ran along the track, grabbing at the freight. It was dawn, cold and gray.

"Wonder where Christ is by now?" Sargeant thought. "He musta gone on way on down the road. He didn't sleep in this jungle."

Sargeant grabbed the train and started to pull himself up into a moving coal car, over the edge of a wheeling coal car. But strangely enough, the car was full of cops. The nearest cop rapped Sargeant soundly across the knuckles with his night stick. Wham! Rapped his big black hands for clinging to the top of the car. Wham! But Sargeant did not turn loose. He clung on and tried to pull himself into the car. He hollered at the top of his voice, "Damn it, lemme in this car!"

"Shut up," barked the cop. "You crazy coon!" He rapped Sargeant across the knuckles and punched him in the stomach. "You ain't out in no jungle now. This ain't no train. You in jail."

Wham! across his bare black fingers clinging to the bars of his cell! Wham! between the steel bars low down against his shins.

Suddenly Sargeant realized that he really was in jail. He wasn't on no train. The blood of the night before had dried on his face, his head hurt terribly, and a cop outside in the corridor was hitting him across the knuckles for holding on to the door, yelling and shaking the cell door.

"They musta took me to jail for breaking down the door last night," Sargeant thought, "that church door."

Sargeant went over and sat on a wooden bench against the cold stone wall. He was emptier than ever. His clothes were wet, clammy cold wet, and shoes sloppy with snow water. It was just about dawn. There he was, locked up behind a cell door, nursing his bruised fingers.

The bruised fingers were his, but not the *door.*

Not the *club,* but the fingers.

"You wait," mumbled Sargeant, black against the jail wall. "I'm gonna break down this door, too."

"Shut up—or I'll paste you one," said the cop.

"I'm gonna break down this door," yelled Sargeant as he stood up in his cell.

Then he must have been talking to himself because he said, "I wonder where Christ's gone? I wonder if he's gone to Kansas City?"

FOR DISCUSSION

1. This story is clearly meant to be symbolic. Describe Sargeant. What is he meant to represent? What do the white people represent?

2. Christ says, "You had to pull the church down to get me off the cross. . . . They have kept me nailed on a cross for nearly two thousand years." What does he mean?

3. There are many references to doors in the story. What do doors represent? Sargeant says at the end, "I'm gonna break down this door." Do you think he will?

Ballad of the Landlord

Landlord, landlord,
My roof has sprung a leak.
Don't you 'member I told you about it
Way last week?

Landlord, landlord,
These steps is broken down.
When you come up yourself,
It's a wonder you don't fall down.

Ten Bucks you say I owe you?
Ten Bucks you say is due?
Well, that's Ten Bucks more'n I'll pay you
Till you fix this house up new.

What? You gonna get eviction orders?
You gonna cut off my heat?
You gonna take my furniture and
Throw it in the street?

Um-huh! You talking high and mighty.
Talk on—till you get through.
You ain't gonna be able to say a word
If I land my fist on you.

Police! Police!
Come and get this man!
He's trying to ruin the government
And overturn the land!

Copper's whistle!
Patrol bell!
Arrest.

Precinct Station.
Iron cell.
Headlines in press:

MAN THREATENS LANDLORD

TENANT HELD NO BAIL

JUDGE GIVES NEGRO 90 DAYS IN COUNTY JAIL

FOR DISCUSSION

1. Who is the speaker in the first five stanzas? What kind of man is he? Who is the speaker in the sixth stanza? How does he react to the words of the first speaker?

2. What does the rest of the poem relate? Why does Hughes make this part of the poem move so rapidly?

3. This poem deals with a serious subject in an amusing way. Why do you think Hughes has chosen this tone?

Crowns and Garlands

Make a garland of Leontynes and Lenas
And hang it about your neck
  Like a lei.
Make a crown of Sammys, Sidneys, Harrys,
Plus Cassius Mohammed Ali Clay.
Put their laurels on your brow
  Today—
Then before you can walk
To the neighborhood corner,
Watch them droop, wilt, fade
  Away.
Though worn in glory on my head,
They do not last a day—
  Not one—
Nor take the place of meat or bread
Or rent that I must pay.
Great names for crowns and garlands!
  Yeah!
I love Ralph Bunche—
But I can't eat him for lunch.

FOR DISCUSSION

How do the last two lines summarize the meaning of the entire
poem?

Melvin B. Tolson

1898–1966

Designated Poet Laureate of Liberia and awarded various prizes, including a fellowship from the Rockefeller Foundation, Melvin Tolson was not recognized as a major poet until the appearance of his last book, Harlem Gallery, *in 1965. His popular poem "Dark Symphony" won the National Poetry Contest conducted by the American Negro Exposition in Chicago and was published in* The Atlantic Monthly. *Tolson was born in Missouri and educated at Fisk, Lincoln, and Columbia Universities. For several decades he taught at Langston University in Oklahoma, where he was Professor of Creative Literature and director of the campus theater. At the time of his death, he was Writer-in-Residence at Tuskegee.*

Dark Symphony

1

Allegro Moderato

Black Crispus Attucks taught
       Us how to die
Before white Patrick Henry's bugle breath

Uttered the vertical
                Transmitting cry:
"Yea, give me liberty or give me death."

Waifs of the auction block,
                Men black and strong
The juggernauts[1] of despotism withstood,
Loin-girt with faith that worms
                Equate the wrong
And dust is purged to create brotherhood.

No Banquo's ghost[2] can rise
                Against us now,
Aver we hobnailed Man beneath the brute,
Squeezed down the thorns of greed
                On Labor's brow,
Garroted lands and carted off the loot.

2

Lento Grave

The centuries-old pathos in our voices
Saddens the great white world,
And the wizardry of our dusky rhythms
Conjures up shadow-shapes of ante-bellum[3] years:

Black slaves singing *One More River to Cross*
In the torture tombs of slave-ships,
Black slaves singing *Steal Away to Jesus*
In jungle swamps,
Black slaves singing *The Crucifixion*

[1] JUGGERNAUTS: in India, idols drawn on huge wagons, said to have
crushed worshippers under their wheels.
[2] BANQUO'S GHOST: In Shakespeare's *Macbeth*, the spirit of a murdered
general confronts the king who ordered his death.
[3] ANTE-BELLUM (ăn'tē-bĕl'əm): Latin for "before the war"; here, pre-
Civil War.

In slave-pens at midnight,
Black slaves singing *Swing Low, Sweet Chariot*
In cabins of death,
Black slaves singing *Go Down, Moses*
In the canebrakes of the Southern Pharaohs.

3

Andante Sostenuto

They tell us to forget
The Golgotha we tread . . .
We who are scourged with hate,
A price upon our head.
They who have shackled us
Require of us a song,
They who have wasted us
Bid us condone the wrong.

They tell us to forget
Democracy is spurned.
They tell us to forget
The Bill of Rights is burned.
Three hundred years we slaved,
We slave and suffer yet:
Though flesh and bone rebel,
They tell us to forget!

Oh, how can we forget
Our human rights denied?
Oh, how can we forget
Our manhood crucified?
When Justice is profaned
And plea with curse is met,
When Freedom's gates are barred,
Oh, how can we forget?

4

Tempo Primo

The New Negro strides upon the continent
In seven-league boots . . .
The New Negro
Who sprang from the vigor-stout loins
Of Nat Turner, gallows-martyr for Freedom,
Of Joseph Cinquez, Black Moses of the Amistad Mutiny,
Of Frederick Douglass, oracle of the Catholic Man,
Of Sojourner Truth, eye and ear of Lincoln's legions,
Of Harriet Tubman, Saint Bernard of the Underground
    Railroad.

The New Negro
Breaks the icons of his detractors,
Wipes out the conspiracy of silence,
Speaks to *his* America:

"My history-moulding ancestors
Planted the first crops of wheat on these shores,
Built ships to conquer the seven seas,
Erected the Cotton Empire,
Flung railroads across a hemisphere,
Disemboweled the earth's iron and coal,
Tunneled the mountains and bridged rivers,
Harvested the grain and hewed forests,
Sentineled the Thirteen Colonies,
Unfurled Old Glory at the North Pole,
Fought a hundred battles for the Republic."

The New Negro:
His giant hands fling murals upon high chambers,
His drama teaches a world to laugh and weep,
His music leads continents captive,
His voice thunders the Brotherhood of Labor,
His science creates seven wonders,
His Republic of Letters challenges the Negro-baiters.

The New Negro,
Hard-muscled, Fascist-hating, Democracy-ensouled,
Strides in seven-league boots
Along the Highway of Today
Toward the Promised Land of Tomorrow!

5

Larghetto

None in the Land can say
To us black men Today:
You send the tractors on their bloody path,
And create Okies for *The Grapes of Wrath.*
You breed the slum that breeds a *Native Son*
To damn the good earth Pilgrim Fathers won.

None in the Land can say
To us black men Today:
You dupe the poor with rags-to-riches tales,
And leave the workers empty dinner pails.
You stuff the ballot box, and honest men
Are muzzled by your demagogic din.

None in the Land can say
To us black men Today:
You smash stock markets with your coined blitzkriegs,
And make a hundred million guinea pigs.
You counterfeit our Christianity,
And bring contempt upon Democracy.

None in the Land can say
To us black men Today:
You prowl when citizens are fast asleep,
And hatch Fifth Column plots to blast the deep
Foundations of the State and leave the Land
A vast Sahara with a Fascist brand.

6

Tempo di Marcia

Out of abysses of Illiteracy,
Through labyrinths of Lies,
Across waste lands of Disease . . .
We advance!

Out of dead-ends of Poverty,
Through wildernesses of Superstition,
Across barricades of Jim Crowism . . .
We advance!

With the Peoples of the World . . .
We advance!

FOR DISCUSSION

1. In this poem there are many literary and historical allusions. Why do you think the poet uses them?

2. What kinds of repetition do you find in section 4? What is the cumulative effect of all the repetition?

3. Why is the poem called a "symphony"?

Richard
Wright

1908–1960

The first major author to deal with the economic frustration of Blacks in the ghetto, Richard Wright had a significant influence on Black writers who have followed him. Born on a farm in Mississippi, Wright spent part of his youth in an orphanage. He later worked at a succession of jobs and suffered humiliation from several white employers. Hoping that "life could be lived with dignity," Wright moved to Chicago in 1927, adopted Marxist ideas, and began to publish poems and essays in radical magazines. During the thirties he rejected his affiliation with the Communist Party. In 1938 he published Uncle Tom's Children, *a collection of stories about sharecroppers in the rural South.* Native Son, *which followed in 1940, dealt with the economic plight of urban Blacks. In voluntary exile from what he considered American racism, Wright spent the last decade of his life in France and England.*

The Man Who Went to Chicago

Christmas came and I was once more called to the post office for temporary work. This time I met many young white men, and we discussed world happenings, the vast armies of unemployed, the rising tide of radical action. I now detected a change in the attitudes of the whites I met; their privations were making them regard Negroes with new eyes, and, for the first time, I was invited to their homes.

When the work in the post office ended, I was assigned by the relief system as an orderly to a medical research institute in one of the largest and wealthiest hospitals in Chicago. I cleaned operating rooms, dog, rat, mice, cat, and rabbit pans, and fed guinea pigs. Four of us Negroes worked there and we occupied an underworld position, remembering that we must restrict ourselves—when not engaged upon some task—to the basement corridors, so that we would not mingle with white nurses, doctors, or visitors.

The sharp line of racial division drawn by the hospital authorities came to me the first morning when I walked along an underground corridor and saw two long lines of women coming toward me. A line of white girls marched past, clad in starched uniforms that gleamed white; their faces were alert, their step quick, their bodies lean and shapely, their shoulders erect, their faces lit with the light of purpose. And after them came a line of black girls, old, fat, dressed in ragged gingham, walking loosely, carrying tin cans of soap powder, rags, mops, brooms.... I wondered what law of the universe kept them from being mixed? The sun would not have stopped shining had there been a few black girls in the first line, and the earth would not have stopped whirling on its axis had there been a few white girls in the second line. But the two lines I saw graded social status in purely racial terms.

Of the three Negroes who worked with me, one was a boy about my own age, Bill, who was either sleepy or drunk most of the time. Bill straightened his hair, and I suspected that he kept a bottle hidden somewhere in the piles of hay which we fed to the guinea pigs. He did not like me and I did not like him, though I tried harder than he to conceal my dislike. We had nothing in common except that we were both black and lost. While I contained my frustration, he drank to drown his. Often I tried to talk to him, tried in simple words to convey to him some of my ideas, and he would listen in sullen silence. Then one day he came to me with an angry look on his face.

"I got it," he said.

"You've got what?" I asked.

"This old race problem you keep talking about," he said.

"What about it?"

"Well, it's this way," he explained seriously. "Let the government give every man a gun and five bullets, then let us all start over again. Make it just like it was in the beginning. The ones who come out on top, white or black, let them rule."

His simplicity terrified me. I had never met a Negro who was so irredeemably brutalized. I stopped pumping my ideas into Bill's brain for fear that the fumes of alcohol might send him reeling toward some fantastic fate.

The two other Negroes were elderly and had been employed in the institute for fifteen years or more. One was Brand, a short, black, morose bachelor; the other was Cooke, a tall, yellow, spectacled fellow who spent his spare time keeping track of world events through the Chicago *Tribune*. Brand and Cooke hated each other for a reason that I was never able to determine, and they spent a good part of each day quarreling.

When I began working at the institute, I recalled my adolescent dream of wanting to be a medical research worker. Daily I saw young Jewish boys and girls receiving instruction in chemistry and medicine that the average black boy or girl could never receive. When I was alone, I wandered and poked my fingers into strange chemicals, watched intricate machines trace red and black lines on ruled paper. At times I paused and stared at the walls of the rooms, at the floors, at the wide desks at which the white doctors sat; and I realized—with a feeling that I could never quite get used to—that I was looking at the world of another race.

My interest in what was happening in the institute amused the three other Negroes with whom I worked. They had no curiosity about "white folks' things," while I wanted to know if the dogs being treated for diabetes were getting

well, if the rats and mice in which cancer had been in-
duced showed any signs of responding to treatment. I
wanted to know the principle that lay behind the Aschheim-
Zondek tests that were made with rabbits, the Wassermann
tests that were made with guinea pigs. But when I asked a
timid question, I found that even Jewish doctors had
learned to imitate the sadistic method of humbling a Negro
that the others had cultivated.

"If you know too much, boy, your brains might explode,"
a doctor said one day.

Each Saturday morning I assisted a young Jewish doctor
in slitting the vocal cords of a fresh batch of dogs from the
city pound. The object was to devocalize the dogs so that
their howls would not disturb the patients in the other
parts of the hospital. I held each dog as the doctor injected
Nembutal into its veins to make it unconscious; then I held
the dog's jaws open as the doctor inserted the scalpel and
severed the vocal cords. Later, when the dogs came to,
they would lift their heads to the ceiling and gape in a
soundless wail. The sight became lodged in my imagination
as a symbol of silent suffering.

To me Nembutal was a powerful and mysterious liquid,
but when I asked questions about its properties, I could not
obtain a single intelligent answer. The doctor simply ignored me with:

"Come on. Bring me the next dog. I haven't got all day."

One Saturday morning, after I had held the dogs for their
vocal cords to be slit, the doctor left the Nembutal on a
bench. I picked it up, uncorked it, and smelled it. It was
odorless. Suddenly Brand ran to me with a stricken face.

"What're you doing?" he asked.

"I was smelling this stuff to see if it had any odor," I said.

"Did you really smell it?" he asked me.

"Yes."

"Oh, God!" he exclaimed.

"What's the matter?" I asked.

"You shouldn't've done that!" he shouted.

"Why?"

He grabbed my arm and jerked me across the room.

"Come on!" he yelled, snatching open the door.

"What's the matter?" I asked.

"I gotta get you to a doctor 'fore it's too late," he gasped.

Had my foolish curiosity made me inhale something dangerous?

"But—is it poisonous?"

"Run, boy!" he said, pulling me. "You'll fall dead."

Filled with fear, with Brand pulling my arm, I rushed out of the room, raced across a rear areaway, into another room, then down a long corridor. I wanted to ask Brand what symptoms I must expect, but we were running too fast. Brand finally stopped, gasping for breath. My heart beat wildly and my blood pounded in my head. Brand then dropped to the concrete floor, stretched out on his back, and yelled with laughter, shaking all over. He beat his fists against the concrete; he moaned, giggled; he kicked.

I tried to master my outrage, wondering if some of the white doctors had told him to play the joke. He rose and wiped tears from his eyes, still laughing. I walked away from him. He knew that I was angry and he followed me.

"Don't get mad," he gasped through his laughter.

"Go to hell," I said.

"I couldn't help it," he giggled. "You looked at me like you'd believe anything I said. Man, you was scared."

He leaned against the wall, laughing again, stomping his feet. I was angry, for I felt that he would spread the story. I knew that Bill and Cooke never ventured beyond the safe bounds of Negro living, and they would never blunder into anything like this. And if they heard about this, they would laugh for months.

"Brand, if you mention this, I'll kill you," I swore.

"You ain't mad?" he asked, laughing, staring at me through tears.

Sniffing, Brand walked ahead of me. I followed him back into the room that housed the dogs. All day, while at some task, he would pause and giggle, then smother the giggling with his hand, looking at me out of the corner of his eyes, shaking his head. He laughed at me for a week. I kept my temper and let him amuse himself. I finally found out the properties of Nembutal by consulting medical books; but I never told Brand.

One summer morning, just as I began work, a young Jewish boy came to me with a stopwatch in his hand.

"Dr. _____ wants me to time you when you clean a room," he said. "We're trying to make the institute more efficient."

"I'm doing my work and getting through on time," I said.

"This is the boss's order," he said.

"Why don't you work for a change?" I blurted, angry.

"Now, look," he said. "*This* is my work. Now *you* work."

I got a mop and pail, sprayed a room with disinfectant, and scrubbed at coagulated blood and hardened dog, rat, and rabbit feces. The normal temperature of a room was ninety, but as the sun beat down upon the skylights, the temperature rose above a hundred. Stripped to my waist, I slung the mop, moving steadily like a machine, hearing the boy press the button on the stopwatch as I finished cleaning a room.

"Well, how is it?" I asked.

"It took you seventeen minutes to clean that last room," he said. "That ought to be the time for each room."

"But that room was not very dirty," I said.

"You have seventeen rooms to clean," he went on as though I had not spoken. "Seventeen times seventeen make four hours and forty-nine minutes." He wrote upon a little pad. "After lunch, clean the five flights of stone stairs. I timed a boy who scrubbed one step and multiplied that time by the number of steps. You ought to be through by six."

"Suppose I want relief?" I asked.

"You'll manage," he said and left.

Never had I felt so much the slave as when I scoured those stone steps each afternoon. Working against time, I would wet five steps, sprinkle soap powder, and then a white doctor or nurse would come along and, instead of avoiding the soapy steps, would walk on them and track the dirty water onto the steps that I had already cleaned. To obviate[1] this, I cleaned but two steps at a time, a distance over which a ten-year-old child could step. But it did no good. The white people still plopped their feet down into the dirty water and muddied the other clean steps. If I ever really hotly hated unthinking whites, it was then. Not once during my entire stay at the institute did a single white person show enough courtesy to avoid a wet step. I would be on my knees, scrubbing, sweating, pouring out what limited energy my body could wring from my meager diet, and I would hear feet approaching. I would pause and curse with tense lips.

Sometimes a sadistically observant white man would notice that he had tracked dirty water up the steps, and he would look back down at me and smile and say:

"Boy, we sure keep you busy, don't we?"

And I would not be able to answer.

The feud that went on between Brand and Cooke continued. Although they were working daily in a building where scientific history was being made, the light of curiosity was never in their eyes. They were conditioned to their racial "place," had learned to see only a part of the whites and the white world; and the whites, too, had learned to see only a part of the lives of the blacks and their world.

Perhaps Brand and Cooke, lacking interests that could absorb them, fuming like children over trifles, simply invented their hate of each other in order to have something to feel deeply about. Or perhaps there was in them a vague tension stemming from their chronically frustrating way of life, a pain whose cause they did not know; and like those devocalized dogs, they would whirl and snap at the air when their old pain struck them. Anyway, they argued about the weather, sports, sex, war, race, politics, and religion; neither of them knew much about the subjects they debated, but it seemed that the less they knew, the better they could argue.

The tug of war between the two elderly men reached a climax one winter day at noon. It was incredibly cold, and

---

[1] OBVIATE (ŏb'vē·āt): prevent, by using forethought.

an icy gale swept up and down the Chicago streets with blizzard force. The door of the animal-filled room was locked, for we always insisted that we be allowed one hour in which to eat and rest. Bill and I were sitting on wooden boxes, eating our lunches out of paper bags. Brand was washing his hands at the sink. Cooke was sitting on a rickety stool, munching an apple and reading the Chicago *Tribune*.

Now and then a devocalized dog lifted his nose to the ceiling and howled soundlessly. The room was filled with many rows of high steel tiers. Perched upon each of these tiers were layers of steel cages containing the dogs, rats, mice, rabbits, and guinea pigs. Each cage was labeled in some indecipherable scientific jargon. Along the walls of the room were long charts with zigzagging red and black lines that traced the success or failure of some experiment. The lonely piping of guinea pigs floated unheeded about us. Hay rustled as a rabbit leaped restlessly about in its pen. A rat scampered around in its steel prison. Cooke tapped the newspaper for attention.

"It says here," Cooke mumbled through a mouthful of apple, "that this is the coldest day since 1888."

Bill and I sat unconcerned. Brand chuckled softly.

"What in hell you laughing about?" Cooke demanded of Brand.

"You can't believe what that damn *Tribune* says," Brand said.

"How come I can't?" Cooke demanded. "It's the world's greatest newspaper."

Brand did not reply; he shook his head pityingly and chuckled again.

"Stop that damn laughing at me!" Cooke said angrily.

"I laugh as much as I wanna," Brand said. "You don't know what you talking about. The *Herald-Examiner* says it's the coldest day since 1873."

"But the *Trib* oughta know," Cooke countered. "It's older'n that *Examiner*."

"That damn *Trib* don't know nothing!" Brand drowned out Cooke's voice.

"How in hell you know?" Cooke asked with rising anger.

The argument waxed until Cooke shouted that if Brand did not shut up he was going to "cut his black throat."

Brand whirled from the sink, his hands dripping soapy water, his eyes blazing.

"Take that back," Brand said.

"I take nothing back! What you wanna do about it?" Cooke taunted.

The two elderly Negroes glared at each other. I wondered if the quarrel was really serious, or if it would turn out harmlessly as so many others had done.

Suddenly Cooke dropped the Chicago *Tribune* and pulled a long knife from his pocket; his thumb pressed a button and a gleaming steel blade leaped out. Brand stepped back quickly and seized an ice pick that was stuck in a wooden board above the sink.

"Put that knife down," Brand said.

"Stay 'way from me, or I'll cut your throat," Cooke warned.

Brand lunged with the ice pick. Cooke dodged out of range. They circled each other like fighters in a prize ring. The cancerous and tubercular rats and mice leaped about in their cages. The guinea pigs whistled in fright. The diabetic dogs bared their teeth and barked soundlessly in our direction. The Aschheim-Zondek rabbits flopped their ears and tried to hide in the corners of their pens. Cooke now crouched and sprang forward with the knife. Bill and I jumped to our feet, speechless with surprise. Brand retreated. The eyes of both men were hard and unblinking; they were breathing deeply.

"Say, cut it out!" I called in alarm.

"Them damn fools is really fighting," Bill said in amazement.

Slashing at each other, Brand and Cooke surged up and down the aisles of steel tiers. Suddenly Brand uttered a bellow and charged into Cooke and swept him violently backward. Cooke grasped Brand's hand to keep the ice pick from sinking into his chest. Brand broke free and charged Cooke again, sweeping him into an animal-filled

steel tier. The tier balanced itself on its edge for an inde-
cisive moment, then toppled.

Like kingpins, one steel tier lammed into another; then
they all crashed to the floor with a sound as of the roof falling. The whole aspect of the room altered quicker than the
eye could follow. Brand and Cooke stood stock-still, their
eyes fastened upon each other, their pointed weapons
raised; but they were dimly aware of the havoc that churned
about them.

The steel tiers lay jumbled; the doors of the cages swung
open. Rats and mice and dogs and rabbits moved over the
floor in wild panic. The Wassermann guinea pigs were
squealing as though judgment day had come. Here and
there an animal had been crushed beneath a cage.

All four of us looked at one another. We knew what this
meant. We might lose our jobs. We were already regarded
as black dunces; and if the doctors saw this mess, they
would take it as final proof. Bill rushed to the door to make
sure that it was locked. I glanced at the clock and saw that it
was 12:30. We had one half hour of grace.

"Come on," Bill said uneasily. "We got to get this place
cleaned."

Brand and Cooke stared at each other, both doubting.

"Give me your knife, Cooke," I said.

"Naw! Take Brand's ice pick *first,*" Cooke said.

"The hell you say!" Brand said. "Take his knife *first!*"

A knock sounded at the door.

"Sssssh," Bill said.

We waited. We heard footsteps going away. We'll all lose
our jobs, I thought.

Persuading the fighters to surrender their weapons was a
difficult task, but at last it was done and we could begin to
set things right. Slowly Brand stooped and tugged at one
end of a steel tier. Cooke stooped to help him. Both men
seemed to be acting in a dream. Soon, however, all four of
us were working frantically, watching the clock.

As we labored, we conspired to keep the fight a secret;
we agreed to tell the doctors—if any should ask—that we
had not been in the room during our lunch hour; we felt

that that lie would explain why no one had unlocked the door when the knock had come.

We righted the tiers and replaced the cages; then we were faced with the impossible task of sorting the cancerous rats and mice, the diabetic dogs, the Aschheim-Zondek rabbits, and the Wassermann guinea pigs. Whether we kept our jobs or not depended upon how shrewdly we could cover up all evidence of the fight. It was pure guesswork, but we had to try to put the animals back into the correct cages. We knew that certain rats or mice went into certain cages, but we did not know *what* rat or mouse went into *what* cage. We did not know a tubercular mouse from a cancerous mouse—the white doctors had made sure that we would not know. They had never taken time to answer a single question; though we worked in the institute, we were as remote from the meaning of the experiments as if we lived in the moon. The doctors had laughed at what they felt was our childlike interest in the fate of the animals.

First we sorted the dogs; that was fairly easy, for we could remember the size and color of most of them. But the rats and mice and guinea pigs baffled us completely.

We put our heads together and pondered, down in the underworld of the great scientific institute. It was a strange scientific conference; the fate of the entire medical research institute rested in our ignorant, black hands.

We remembered the number of rats, mice, or guinea pigs—we had to handle them several times a day—that went into a given cage, and we supplied the number helter-skelter from those animals that we could catch running loose on the floor. We discovered that many rats, mice, and guinea pigs were missing—they had been killed in the scuffle. We solved that problem by taking healthy stock from other cages and putting them into cages with sick animals. We repeated this process until we were certain that, numerically at least, all the animals with which the doctors were experimenting were accounted for.

The rabbits came last. We broke the rabbits down into two general groups; those that had fur on their bellies and those that did not. We knew that all those rabbits that had shaven bellies—our scientific knowledge adequately covered this point because it was our job to shave the rabbits—were undergoing the Aschheim-Zondek tests. But in what pen did a given rabbit belong? We did not know. I solved the problem very simply. I counted the shaven rabbits; they numbered seventeen. I counted the pens labeled "Aschheim-Zondek," then proceeded to drop a shaven rabbit into each pen at random. And again we were numerically successful. At least white America had taught us how to count. . . .

Lastly we carefully wrapped all the dead animals in newspapers and hid their bodies in a garbage can.

At a few minutes to one the room was in order; that is, the kind of order that we four Negroes could figure out. I unlocked the door and we sat waiting, whispering, vowing secrecy, wondering what the reaction of the doctors would be.

Finally a doctor came, gray-haired, white-coated, spectacled, efficient, serious, taciturn, bearing a tray upon which sat a bottle of mysterious fluid and a hypodermic needle.

"My rats, please."

Cooke shuffled forward to serve him. We held our breath. Cooke got the cage which he knew the doctor always called for at that hour and brought it forward. One by one, Cooke took out the rats and held them as the doctor solemnly injected the mysterious fluid under their skins.

"Thank you, Cooke," the doctor murmured.

"Not at all, sir," Cooke mumbled with a suppressed gasp.

When the doctor had gone, we looked at one another, hardly daring to believe that our secret would be kept. We were so anxious that we did not know whether to curse or laugh. Another doctor came.

"Give me A-Z rabbit number 14."

"Yes, sir," I said.

I brought him the rabbit, and he took it upstairs to the operating room. We waited for repercussions. None came.

All that afternoon the doctors came and went. I would run into the room—stealing a few seconds from my step-scrubbing—and ask what progress was being made and would learn that the doctors had detected nothing. At quitting time we felt triumphant.

"They won't ever know," Cooke boasted in a whisper.

I saw Brand stiffen. I knew that he was aching to dispute Cooke's optimism, but the memory of the fight he had just had was so fresh in his mind that he could not speak.

Another day went by and nothing happened. Then another day. The doctors examined the animals and wrote in their little black books, in their big black books, and continued to trace red and black lines upon the charts.

A week passed and we felt out of danger. Not one question had been asked.

Of course, we four black men were much too modest to make our contribution known, but we often wondered what went on in the laboratories after that secret disaster. Was some scientific hypothesis, well on its way to validation and ultimate public use, discarded because of unexpected findings on that cold winter day? Was some tested principle given a new and strange refinement because of fresh, remarkable evidence? Did some brooding research worker— those who held stopwatches and slopped their feet carelessly in the water of the steps I tried so hard to keep clean —get a wild, if brief, glimpse of a new scientific truth? Well, we never heard. . . .

I brooded upon whether I should have gone to the director's office and told him what had happened, but each time I thought of it, I remembered that the director had been the man who had ordered the boy to stand over me while I was working and time my movements with a stopwatch. He did not regard me as a human being. I did not share his world. I earned thirteen dollars a week and I had to support four people with it, and should I risk that thirteen dollars by acting idealistically? Brand and Cooke would have hated me and would have eventually driven me from the job had I "told" on them. The hospital kept us four Negroes as though we were close kin to the animals we tended, huddled together down in the underworld corridors of the hospital, separated by a vast psychological distance from the significant processes of the rest of the hospital—just as America had kept us locked in the dark underworld of American life for three hundred years—and we had made our own code of ethics, values, loyalty.

FOR DISCUSSION

1. In this selection, Wright describes a hospital divided into two "worlds": the basement "underworld" and the "world" of the building above. What is life like in each of these worlds? What do the two worlds symbolize?

2. What effect does the "underworld" have on the people who live in it? Does it have similar effects on each of the characters?

3. After the fight, the Black men return the animals to the wrong cages, and the white researchers never know the difference. What is Wright satirizing in this episode?

Ralph Ellison

b. 1914

Best known for Invisible Man, *his novel which won the National Book Award in 1952, Ralph Ellison has also written several short stories and a book of essays entitled* Shadow and Act. *In all of his writing, Ellison dramatizes the need for white America to recognize the complex identity of the Black man. Ellison's is a voice of protest, but his tone is idealistic and optimistic; he stresses pride in Black identity and freedom. "If I cannot look at the most brutalized Negro on the street, even when he irritates me and makes me want to bash his head in because he's goofing off, I must still say within myself, 'Well, that's you too, Ellison.' And I'm not talking about guilt, but of an identification which goes beyond race." Ellison, who taught at Barnard and Bennington Colleges, has been a writer-in-residence at Rutgers, a visiting fellow at Yale, and a lecturer at the State University of New York at Stony Brook.*

King of the Bingo Game

The woman in front of him was eating roasted peanuts that smelled so good that he could barely contain his hunger. He could not even sleep and wished they'd hurry and begin the bingo game. There, on his right, two fellows were drinking wine out of a bottle wrapped in a paper bag, and he could hear soft gurgling in the dark. His stomach gave a low, gnawing growl. If this was down South, he thought, all I'd have to do is lean over and say, "Lady, gimme a few of those peanuts, please ma'am," and she'd pass me the bag and never think nothing of it. Or he could ask the fellows for a drink in the same way. Folks down South stuck together that way; they didn't even have to know you. But up here it was different. Ask somebody for something, and they'd think you were crazy. Well, I ain't crazy. I'm just broke, 'cause I got no birth certificate to get a job, and Laura 'bout to die 'cause we got no money for a doctor. But I ain't crazy. And yet a pinpoint of doubt was focused in his mind as he glanced toward the screen and saw the hero stealthily entering a dark room and sending the beam of a flashlight along a wall of bookcases. This is where he finds the trap-door, he remembered. The man would pass abruptly through the wall and find the girl tied to a bed, her legs and arms spread wide, and her clothing torn to rags. He laughed softly to himself. He had seen the picture three times, and this was one of the best scenes.

On his right the fellow whispered wide-eyed to his companion, "Man, look a-yonder!"

"Damn!"

"Wouldn't I like to have her tied up like that. . . ."

"Hey! That fool's letting her loose!"

"Aw, man, he loves her."

"Love or no love!"

The man moved impatiently beside him, and he tried to involve himself in the scene. But Laura was on his mind. Tiring quickly of watching the picture, he looked back to where the white beam filtered from the projection room above the balcony. It started small and grew large, specks of dust dancing in its whiteness as it reached the screen. It was strange how the beam always landed right on the screen and didn't mess up and fall somewhere else. But they had it all fixed. Everything was fixed. Now suppose when they showed that girl with her dress torn, the girl started taking off the rest of her clothes, and when the guy came in, he didn't untie her but kept her there and went to taking off his own clothes? *That* would be something to see. If a picture got out of hand like that, those guys up there would go nuts. Yeah, and there'd be so many folks in here you couldn't find a seat for nine months! A strange sensation played over his skin. He shuddered. Yesterday he'd seen a bedbug on a woman's neck as they walked out into the bright street. But exploring his thigh through a hole in his pocket, he found only goose pimples and old scars.

The bottle gurgled again. He closed his eyes. Now a dreamy music was accompanying the film, and train whistles were sounding in the distance, and he was a boy again walking along a railroad trestle down South, and seeing the train coming, and running back as fast as he could go, and hearing the whistle blowing, and getting off the trestle to solid ground just in time, with the earth trembling beneath his feet, and feeling relieved as he ran down the cinder-strewn embankment onto the highway, and looking back and seeing with terror that the train had left the track and was following him right down the middle of the street, and all the white people laughing as he ran screaming. . . .

"Wake up there, buddy! What the hell do you mean hollering like that? Can't you see we trying to enjoy this here picture?"

He stared at the man with gratitude.

"I'm sorry, old man," he said. "I musta been dreaming."

"Well, here, have a drink. And don't be making no noise like that, damn!"

His hands trembled as he tilted his head. It was not wine, but whiskey. Cold rye whiskey. He took a deep swoller, decided it was better not to take another, and handed the bottle back to its owner.

"Thanks, old man," he said.

Now he felt the cold whiskey breaking a warm path straight through the middle of him, growing hotter and sharper as it moved. He had not eaten all day, and it made him light-headed. The smell of the peanuts stabbed him like a knife, and he got up and found a seat in the middle aisle. But no sooner did he sit than he saw a row of intense-faced young girls and got up again, thinking, You chicks musta been Lindy-hopping somewhere. He found a seat several rows ahead as the lights came on, and he saw the screen disappear behind a heavy red and gold curtain, then the curtain rising, and the man with the microphone and a uniformed attendant coming on the stage.

He felt for his bingo cards, smiling. The guy at the door wouldn't like it if he knew about his having *five* cards. Well, not everyone played the bingo game; and even with five cards he didn't have much of a chance. For Laura, though, he had to have faith. He studied the cards, each with its different numerals, punching the free center hole in each and spreading them neatly across his lap; and when the lights faded, he sat slouched in his seat so that he could look from his cards to the bingo wheel with but a quick shifting of his eyes.

Ahead, at the end of the darkness, the man with the microphone was pressing a button attached to a long cord and spinning the bingo wheel and calling out the number each time the wheel came to rest. And each time the voice rang out, his finger raced over the cards for the number. With five cards he had to move fast. He became nervous; there were too many cards, and the man went too fast with his grating voice. Perhaps he should just select one and throw the others away. But he was afraid. He became warm. Wonder how much Laura's doctor would cost? Damn that, watch the cards! And with despair he heard the man call three in a row which he missed on all five cards. This way he'd never win. . . .

When he saw the row of holes punched across the third card, he sat paralyzed and heard the man call three more numbers before he stumbled forward, screaming,

"Bingo! Bingo!"

"Let that fool up there," someone called.

"Get up there, man!"

He stumbled down the aisle and up the steps to the stage into a light so sharp and bright that for a moment it blinded him, and he felt that he had moved into the spell of some strange, mysterious power. Yet it was as familiar as the sun, and he knew it was the perfectly familiar bingo.

The man with the microphone was saying something to the audience as he held out his card. A cold light flashed from the man's finger as the card left his hand. His knees trembled. The man stepped closer, checking the card against the numbers chalked on the board. Suppose he had made a mistake? The pomade on the man's hair made him feel faint, and he backed away. But the man was checking the card over the microphone now, and he had to stay. He stood tense, listening.

"Under the O, forty-four," the man chanted. "Under the I, seven. Under the G, three. Under the B, ninety-six. Under the N, thirteen!"

His breath came easier as the man smiled at the audience.

"Yessir, ladies and gentlemen, he's one of the chosen people!"

The audience rippled with laughter and applause.

"Step right up to the front of the stage."

He moved slowly forward, wishing that the light was not so bright.

"To win tonight's jackpot of $36.90 the wheel must stop between the double zero, understand?"

He nodded, knowing the ritual from the many days and nights he had watched the winners march across the stage to press the button that controlled the spinning wheel and receive the prizes. And now he followed the instructions as though he'd crossed the slippery stage a million prize-winning times.

The man was making some kind of a joke, and he nodded vacantly. So tense had he become that he felt a sudden desire to cry and shook it away. He felt vaguely that his whole life was determined by the bingo wheel; not only that which would happen now that he was at last before it, but all that had gone before, since his birth, and his mother's birth, and the birth of his father. It had always been there, even though he had not been aware of it, handing out the unlucky cards and numbers of his days. The feeling persisted, and he started quickly away. I better get down from here before I make a fool of myself, he thought.

"Here, boy," the man called. "You haven't started yet."

Someone laughed as he went hesitantly back.

"Are you all reet?"

He grinned at the man's jive talk, but no words would come, and he knew it was not a convincing grin. For suddenly he knew that he stood on the slippery brink of some terrible embarrassment.

"Where are you from, boy?" the man asked.

"Down South."

"He's from down South, ladies and gentlemen," the man said. "Where from? Speak right into the mike."

"Rocky Mont," he said. "Rock' Mont, North Car'lina."

"So you decided to come down off that mountain to the U.S.," the man laughed. He felt that the man was making a fool of him, but then something cold was placed in his hand, and the lights were no longer behind him.

Standing before the wheel he felt alone, but that was somehow right, and he remembered his plan. He would give the wheel a short quick twirl. Just a touch of the button. He had watched it many times, and always it came close to double zero when it was short and quick. He steeled himself; the fear had left, and he felt a profound sense of promise, as though he were about to be repaid for all the things he'd suffered all his life. Trembling, he pressed the button. There was a whirl of lights, and in a second he realized with finality that though he wanted to, he could not stop. It was as though he held a high-powered line in his naked hand. His nerves tightened. As the wheel increased its speed, it seemed to draw him more and more into its power, as though it held his fate; and with it came a deep need to submit, to whirl, to lose himself in its swirl of color. He could not stop it now, he knew. So let it be.

The button rested snugly in his palm where the man had placed it. And now he became aware of the man beside him, advising him through the microphone, while behind the shadowy audience hummed with noisy voices. He shifted his feet. There was still that feeling of helplessness within him, making part of him desire to turn back, even now that the jackpot was right in his hand. He squeezed the button until his fist ached. Then, like the sudden shriek of a subway whistle, a doubt tore through his head. Suppose he did not spin the wheel long enough? What could he do, and how could he tell? And then he knew, even as he wondered, that as long as he pressed the button, he could control the jackpot. He and only he could determine whether or not it was to be his. Not even the man with the microphone could do anything about it now. He felt drunk. Then, as though he had come down from a high hill into a valley of people, he heard the audience yelling.

"Come down from there, you jerk!"

"Let somebody else have a chance. . . ."

"Ole Jack thinks he done found the end of the rain-bow. . . ."

The last voice was not unfriendly, and he turned and smiled dreamily into the yelling mouths. Then he turned his back squarely on them.

"Don't take too long, boy," a voice said.

He nodded. They were yelling behind him. Those folks did not understand what had happened to him. They had been playing the bingo game day in and night out for years, trying to win rent money or hamburger change. But not one of those wise guys had discovered this wonderful thing. He watched the wheel whirling past the numbers and experienced a burst of exaltation: This is God! This is the really truly God! He said it aloud, "This is God!"

He said it with such absolute conviction that he feared he would fall fainting into the footlights. But the crowd yelled so loud that they could not hear. Those fools, he thought. I'm here trying to tell them the most wonderful secret in the world, and they're yelling like they gone crazy. A hand fell upon his shoulder.

"You'll have to make a choice now, boy. You've taken too long."

He brushed the hand violently away.

"Leave me alone, man. I know what I'm doing!"

The man looked surprised and held on to the microphone for support. And because he did not wish to hurt the man's feelings, he smiled, realizing with a sudden pang that there was no way of explaining to the man just why he had to stand there pressing the button forever.

"Come here," he called tiredly.

The man approached, rolling the heavy microphone across the stage.

"Anybody can play this bingo game, right?" he said.

"Sure, but. . . ."

He smiled, feeling inclined to be patient with this slick-looking white man with his blue sport shirt and his sharp gabardine suit.

"That's what I thought," he said. "Anybody can win the jackpot as long as they get the lucky number, right?"

"That's the rule, but after all. . . ."

"That's what I thought," he said. "And the big prize goes to the man who knows how to win it?"

The man nodded speechlessly.

"Well then, go on over there and watch me win like I want to. I ain't going to hurt nobody," he said, "and I'll show you how to win. I mean to show the whole world how it's got to be done."

And because he understood, he smiled again to let the man know that he held nothing against him for being white and impatient. Then he refused to see the man any longer and stood pressing the button, the voices of the crowd reaching him like sounds in distant streets. Let them yell. All the Negroes down there were just ashamed because he was black like them. He smiled inwardly, knowing how it was. Most of the time he was ashamed of what Negroes did himself. Well, let them be ashamed for something this time. Like him. He was like a long thin black wire that was being stretched and wound upon the bingo wheel; wound until he wanted to scream; wound, but this time himself controlling the winding and the sadness and the shame, and because he did, Laura would be all right. Suddenly the lights flickered. He staggered backwards. Had something gone wrong? All this noise. Didn't they know that although he controlled the wheel, it also controlled him, and unless he pressed the button forever and forever and ever, it would stop, leaving him high and dry, dry and high on this hard high slippery hill and Laura dead? There was only one chance; he had to do whatever the wheel demanded. And gripping the button in despair, he discovered with surprise that it imparted a nervous energy. His spine tingled. He felt a certain power.

Now he faced the raging crowd with defiance, its screams penetrating his eardrums like trumpets shrieking from a jukebox. The vague faces glowing in the bingo lights gave him a sense of himself that he had never known before. He was running the show, by God! They had to react to him, for he was their luck. This is *me*, he thought. Let the bastards yell. Then someone was laughing inside him, and he realized that somehow he had forgotten his own name. It was a sad, lost feeling to lose your name, and a crazy thing to do. That name had been given him by the white man who had owned his grandfather a long lost time ago down South. But maybe those wise guys knew his name.

"Who am I?" he screamed.

"Hurry up and bingo, you jerk!"

They didn't know either, he thought sadly. They didn't even know their own names; they were all poor nameless bastards. Well, he didn't need that old name; he was reborn. For as long as he pressed the button, he was The-man-who-pressed-the-button-who-held-the-prize-who-was-the-King-of-Bingo. That was the way it was, and he'd have to press the button even if nobody understood, even though Laura did not understand.

"Live!" he shouted.

The audience quieted like the dying of a huge fan.

"Live, Laura, baby. I got holt of it now, sugar. Live!"

He screamed it, tears streaming down his face. "I got nobody but YOU!"

The screams tore from his very guts. He felt as though the rush of blood to his head would burst out in baseball seams of small red droplets, like a head beaten by police clubs. Bending over he saw a trickle of blood splashing the toe of his shoe. With his free hand he searched his head. It was his nose. God, suppose something has gone wrong? He felt that the whole audience had somehow entered him and was stamping its feet in his stomach, and he was unable to throw them out. They wanted the prize; that was it. They wanted the secret for themselves. But they'd never get it; he would keep the bingo wheel whirling forever, and Laura would be safe in the wheel. But would she? It had to be, because if she were not safe, the wheel would cease to turn; it could not go on. He had to get away, *vomit* all, and his mind formed an image of himself running with Laura in his arms down the tracks of the subway just ahead of an A train, running desperately *vomit* with people screaming for him to come out but knowing no way of leaving the tracks because to stop would bring the train crushing down upon him, and to attempt to leave across the other tracks would mean to run into a hot third rail as high as his waist which threw blue sparks that blinded his eyes until he could hardly see.

He heard singing and the audience was clapping its hands.

> "Shoot the liquor to him, Jim, boy!
> Clap-clap-clap
> Well a-calla the cop
> He's blowing his top!
> Shoot the liquor to him, Jim, boy!"

Bitter anger grew within him at the singing. They think I'm crazy. Well, let 'em laugh. I'll do what I got to do.

He was standing in an attitude of intense listening when he saw that they were watching something on the stage behind him. He felt weak. But when he turned, he saw no one. If only his thumb did not ache so. Now they were applauding. And for a moment he thought that the wheel had stopped. But that was impossible; his thumb still pressed the button. Then he saw them. Two men in uniform beckoned from the end of the stage. They were coming toward him, walking in step, slowly, like a tap-dance team returning for a third encore. But their shoulders shot forward, and he backed away, looking wildly about. There was nothing to fight them with. He had only the long black cord which led to a plug somewhere backstage, and he couldn't use that, because it operated the bingo wheel. He backed slowly, fixing the men with his eyes as his lips stretched over his teeth in a tight, fixed grin; moved toward the end of the stage and realizing that he couldn't go much further, for suddenly the cord became taut, and he couldn't afford to break the cord. But he had to do something. The audience was howling. Suddenly he stopped dead, seeing the men halt, their legs lifted as in an interrupted step of a slow-motion dance. There was nothing to do but run in the other direction, and he dashed forward, slipping and sliding. The men fell back, surprised. He struck out violently going past.

"Grab him!"

He ran, but all too quickly the cord tightened, resistingly, and he turned and ran back again. This time he slipped them, and discovered by running in a circle before the wheel he could keep the cord from tightening. But this way he had to flail his arms to keep the men away. Why couldn't they leave a man alone? He ran, circling.

"Ring down the curtain," someone yelled. But they couldn't do that. If they did, the wheel flashing from the projection room would be cut off. But they had him before he could tell them so, trying to pry open his fist, and he was wrestling and trying to bring his knees into the fight and holding on to the button, for it was his life. And now he was down, seeing a foot coming down, crushing his wrist cruelly, down, as he saw the wheel whirling serenely above.

"I can't give it up," he screamed. Then quietly, in a confidential tone, "Boys, I really can't give it up."

It landed hard against his head. And in the blank moment they had it away from him, completely now. He fought them trying to pull him up from the stage as he watched the wheel spin slowly to a stop. Without surprise he saw it rest at double zero.

"You see," he pointed bitterly.

"Sure, boy, sure, it's O.K.," one of the men said smiling.

And seeing the man bow his head to someone he could not see, he felt very, very happy; he would receive what all the winners received.

But as he warmed in the justice of the man's tight smile, he did not see the man's slow wink, nor see the bow-legged man behind him step clear of the swiftly descending curtain and set himself for a blow. He only felt the dull pain exploding in his skull, and he knew even as it slipped out of him that his luck had run out on the stage.

FOR DISCUSSION

1. What do the hero and the bingo wheel symbolize in this story?

2. Twice (pages 62 and 69) the hero imagines that he is being pursued by a train that he cannot escape. How are these passages related to the meaning of the story as a whole?

3. Why does Ellison make the main character of the story a Black man and the master of ceremonies white?

Arna Bontemps

b. 1902

One of the best-known poets of the Harlem Renaissance, Arna Bontemps later turned to writing prose fiction and nonfiction. In his capacity as anthologist, critic, biographer, and teacher as well as writer, he has played a central role in the history of Black literature in the twentieth century. Born in Louisiana and educated at Pacific Union College and the University of Chicago, Bontemps held a variety of teaching positions before assuming the position of chief librarian at Fisk University, which he held for twenty-two years. His own works include Personals, *a collection of his poems;* Black Thunder, *a novel; and* The Story of the Negro, *a historical account. He is currently teaching at the Chicago Circle campus of the University of Chicago.*

Southern Mansion

Poplars are standing there still as death
and ghosts of dead men
meet their ladies walking
two by two beneath the shade
and standing on the marble steps.

There is a sound of music echoing
through the open door

and in the field there is
another sound tinkling in the cotton:
chains of bondmen dragging on the ground.

The years go back with an iron clank,
a hand is on the gate,
a dry leaf trembles on the wall.
Ghosts are walking.
They have broken roses down
and poplars stand there still as death.

FOR DISCUSSION

1. Who are the dead men described in the first stanza? What kind of lives did they lead?

2. Describe the sounds in stanza 2 and explain how they are related.

3. What mood do the visual images of stanza 3 create?

The Day-breakers

We are not come to wage a strife
with swords upon this hill:
it is not wise to waste the life
against a stubborn will.

Yet would we die as some have done:
beating a way for the rising sun.

FOR DISCUSSION

1. How is the meaning of the title clarified in the final couplet?
What does the "rising sun" symbolize?

2. To whom does the speaker refer when he says "We"?

A Black Man Talks of Reaping

I have sown beside all waters in my day.
I planted deep, within my heart the fear
That wind or fowl would take the grain away.
I planted safe against this stark, lean year.

I scattered seed enough to plant the land
In rows from Canada to Mexico,
But for my reaping only what the hand
Can hold at once is all that I can show.

Yet what I sowed and what the orchard yields
My brother's sons are gathering stalk and root,
Small wonder then my children glean in fields
They have not sown, and feed on bitter fruit.

FOR DISCUSSION

What is symbolized by the reaping that the Black man speaks of?
Who are his "brother's sons"?

Gwendolyn Brooks

b. 1917

Winner of the Pulitzer Prize in 1950 for her volume of poetry Annie Allen, *Gwendolyn Brooks has been writing poetry "since about seven, at which time my parents expressed most earnest confidence that I would one day be a writer." Her poems were first published in magazines, when she was only fourteen. Since that time she has received numerous honors and awards for her writing, including the official title Poet Laureate of Illinois, once held by Carl Sandburg. The first Black person to be awarded the Pulitzer Prize, Miss Brooks has written a novel,* Maud Martha, *as well as other volumes of poetry which include* A Street in Bronzeville, Bronzeville Boys and Girls, *and* In the Mecca. *Miss Brooks feels that every Negro writer "because he is a Negro cannot escape having important things to say."*

At the Burns-Coopers'

It was a little red and white and black woman who appeared in the doorway of the beautiful house in Winnetka.

About, thought Maud Martha, thirty-four.

"I'm Mrs. Burns-Cooper," said the woman, "and after this, well, it's all right this time, because it's your first time, but after this time always use the back entrance."

There is a pear in my icebox, and one end of rye bread. Except for three Irish potatoes and a cup of flour and the empty Christmas boxes, there is absolutely nothing on my shelf. My husband is laid off. There is newspaper on my kitchen table instead of oilcloth. I can't find a filing job in a hurry. I'll smile at Mrs. Burns-Cooper and hate her just some.

"First, you have the beds to make," said Mrs. Burns-Cooper. "You either change the sheets or air the old ones for ten minutes. I'll tell you about the changing when the time comes. It isn't any special day. You are to pull my sheets, and pat and pat and pull till all's tight and smooth. Then shake the pillows into the slips, carefully. Then punch them in the middle.

"Next, there is the washing of the midnight snack dishes. Next, there is the scrubbing. Now, I know that your other ladies have probably wanted their floors scrubbed after dinner. I'm different. I like to enjoy a bright clean floor all the day. You can just freshen it up a little before you leave in the evening, if it needs a few more touches. Another thing. I disapprove of mops. You can do a better job on your knees.

"Next is dusting. Next is vacuuming—that's for Tuesdays and Fridays. On Wednesdays, ironing and silver cleaning.

"Now about cooking. You're very fortunate in that here you have only the evening meal to prepare. Neither of us has breakfast, and I always step out for lunch. Isn't that lucky?"

"It's quite a kitchen, isn't it?" Maud Martha observed. "I mean, big."

Mrs. Burns-Cooper's brows raced up in amazement.

"Really? I hadn't thought so. I'll bet"—she twinkled indulgently—"you're comparing it to your *own* little kitchen." And why do that, her light eyes laughed. Why talk of beautiful mountains and grains of alley sand in the same breath?

"Once," mused Mrs. Burns-Cooper, "I had a girl who botched up the kitchen. Made a botch out of it. But all I had to do was just sort of cock my head and say, 'Now, now,

Albertine!' Her name was Albertine. Then she'd giggle and scrub and scrub, and she was *so* sorry about trying to take advantage."

It was while Maud Martha was peeling potatoes for dinner that Mrs. Burns-Cooper laid herself out to prove that she was not a snob. Then it was that Mrs. Burns-Cooper came out to the kitchen and, sitting, talked and talked at Maud Martha. In my college days. At the time of my debut. The imported lace on my lingerie. My brother's rich wife's Stradivarius. When I was in Madrid. The charm of the Nile. Cost fifty dollars. Cost one hundred dollars. Cost one thousand dollars. Shall I mention, considered Maud Martha, my own social triumphs, my own education, my travels to Gary and Milwaukee and Columbus, Ohio? Shall I mention my collection of fancy pink satin bras? She decided against it. She went on listening, in silence, to the confidences until the arrival of the lady's mother-in-law (large-eyed, strong, with hair of a mighty white, and with an eloquent, angry bosom). Then the junior Burns-Cooper was very much the mistress, was stiff, cool, authoritative.

There was no introduction, but the elder Burns-Cooper boomed, "Those potato parings are entirely too thick!"

The two of them, richly dressed, and each with that health in the face that bespeaks, or seems to bespeak, much milk drinking from earliest childhood, looked at Maud Martha. There was no remonstrance; no firing! They just looked. But for the first time, she understood what Paul endured daily. For so—she could gather from a Paul-word here, a Paul-curse there—his Boss! when, squared, upright, terribly upright, superior to the President, commander of the world, he wished to underline Paul's lacks, to indicate soft shock, controlled incredulity. As his boss looked at Paul, so these people looked at her. As though she were a child, a ridiculous one, and one that ought to be given a little shaking, except that shaking was—not quite the thing, would not quite do. One held up one's finger (if one did anything), cocked one's head, was arch. As in the old song, one hinted, "Tut tut! now now! come come!" Metal rose, all built, in one's eye.

I'll never come back, Maud Martha assured herself, when she hung up her apron at eight in the evening. She knew Mrs. Burns-Cooper would be puzzled. The wages were very good. Indeed, what could be said in explanation? Perhaps that the hours were long. I couldn't explain *my* explanation, she thought.

One walked out from that almost perfect wall, spitting at the firing squad. What difference did it make whether the firing squad understood or did not understand the manner of one's retaliation or why one had to retaliate?

Why, one was a human being. One wore clean nightgowns. One loved one's baby. One drank cocoa by the fire— or the gas range—come the evening, in the wintertime.

FOR DISCUSSION

Why does Maud Martha find Mrs. Burns-Cooper and her mother-in-law intolerable? What does she mean when she suggests that leaving the Burns-Coopers' is like "spitting at the firing squad"?

Kitchenette Building

We are things of dry hours and the involuntary plan,
Grayed in, and gray. "Dream" makes a giddy sound, not
strong
Like "rent," "feeding a wife," "satisfying a man."

But could a dream send up through onion fumes
Its white and violet, fight with fried potatoes
And yesterday's garbage ripening in the hall,
Flutter, or sing an aria down these rooms

Even if we were willing to let it in,
Had time to warm it, keep it very clean,
Anticipate a message, let it begin?

We wonder. But not well! not for a minute!
Since Number Five is out of the bathroom now,
We think of lukewarm water, hope to get in it.

FOR DISCUSSION

1. What do the words *things*, *dry*, and *gray* in the first stanza suggest about the inhabitants of the building?

2. Why is it impossible for a dream to enter the speaker's world?

Medgar Evers

For Charles Evers

The man whose height his fear improved he
arranged to fear no further. The raw
intoxicated time was time for better birth or
a final death.

Old styles, old tempos, all the engagement of
the day—the sedate, the regulated fray—
the antique light, the Moral rose, old gusts,
tight whistlings from the past, the mothballs
in the Love at last our man forswore.

Medgar Evers annoyed confetti and assorted
brands of businessmen's eyes.

The shows came down: to maxims and surprise.
And palsy.

Roaring no rapt arise-ye to the dead, he
leaned across tomorrow. People said that
he was holding clean globes in his hands.

FOR DISCUSSION

1. This poem develops a contrast between two worlds, the old
and the new. Describe as precisely as you can the characteristics
of both worlds.

2. What qualities of Medgar Evers does this poem emphasize?

John Oliver Killens

b. 1916

John Oliver Killens, who presently teaches a course in Black culture and directs a creative-writing workshop at Columbia University, hopes in his writing "to debrainwash" Black people about their role in American life. "We have to undo the millions of little white lies that America told itself and the world about the American Black man," he has commented. Killens satirizes the Black bourgeoisie as well as white hypocrisy; in his latest book, The Cotillion, *he criticizes Black men who have accepted the values imposed by white society. Killens has written several other novels, including* Youngblood, And Then We Heard the Thunder, *and* Sippi. *He is the author of a nonfiction book,* Black Man's Burden; *a play,* Lower Than Angels; *and two screenplays,* Odds Against Tomorrow, *starring Harry Belafonte, and* The Slaves, *starring Ossie Davis and Dionne Warwick.*

God Bless America

Joe's dark eyes searched frantically for Cleo as he marched with the other Negro soldiers up the long thoroughfare towards the boat. Women were running out to the line of march, crying and laughing and kissing the men good-bye. But where the hell was Cleo?

82

Beside him Luke Robinson, big and fat, nibbled from a carton of Baby Ruth candy as he walked. But Joe's eyes kept traveling up and down the line of civilians on either side of the street. She would be along here somewhere; any second now she would come calmly out of the throng and walk alongside him till they reached the boat. Joe's mind made a picture of her, and she looked the same as last night when he left her. As he had walked away, with the brisk California night air biting into his warm body, he had turned for one last glimpse of her in the doorway, tiny and smiling and waving good-bye.

They had spent last night sitting in the little two-by-four room where they had lived for three months with hardly enough space to move around. He had rented it and sent for her when he came to California and learned that his outfit was training for immediate shipment to Korea, and they had lived there fiercely and desperately, like they were trying to live a whole lifetime. But last night they had sat on the side of the big iron bed, making conversation, half listening to a portable radio, acting like it was just any night. Play-acting like in the movies.

It was late in the evening when he asked her, "How's little Joey acting lately?"

She looked down at herself. "Oh, pal Joey is having himself a ball." She smiled, took Joe's hand, and placed it on her belly; and he felt movement and life. His and her life, and he was going away from it and from her, maybe forever.

Cleo said, "He's trying to tell you good-bye, darling." And she sat very still and seemed to ponder over her own words. And then all of a sudden she burst into tears.

She was in his arms, and her shoulders shook. "It isn't fair! Why can't they take the ones that aren't married?"

He hugged her tight, feeling a great fullness in his throat. "Come on now, stop crying, hon. Cut it out, will you? I'll be back home before little Joey sees daylight."

"You may never come back. They're killing a lot of our boys over there. Oh, Joe, Joe, why did they have to go and start another war?"

In a gruff voice he said, "Don't you go worrying about Big Joey. He'll take care of himself. You just take care of little Joey and Cleo. That's what you do."

"Don't take any chances, Joe. Don't be a hero!"

He forced himself to laugh and hugged her tighter. "Don't you worry about the mule going blind."

She made herself stop crying and wiped her face. "But I don't understand, Joe. I don't understand what colored soldiers have to fight for—especially against other colored people."

"Honey," said Joe gently, "we got to fight like anybody else. We can't just sit on the sidelines."

But she just looked at him and shook her head.

"Look," he said, "when I get back, I'm going to finish college. I'm going to be a lawyer. That's what I'm fighting for."

She kept shaking her head as if she didn't hear him. "I don't know, Joe. Maybe it's because we were brought up kind of different, you and I. My father died when I was four. My mother worked all her life in white folks' kitchens. I just did make it through high school. You had it a whole lot better than most Negro boys." She went over to the box of Kleenex and blew her nose.

"I don't see where that has a thing to do with it."

He stared at her, angry with her for being so obstinate. Couldn't she see any progress at all? Look at Jackie Robinson. Look at Ralph Bunche. Damn it! they'd been over it all before. What did she want him to do about it anyway? Become a deserter?

She stood up over him. "Can't see it, Joe—just can't see it! I want you here, Joe. Here with me where you belong. Don't leave me, Joe! Please—" She was crying now. "Joe, Joe, what're we going to do? Maybe it would be better to get rid of little Joey—" Her brown eyes were wide with terror. "No, Joe, no! I didn't mean that! I didn't mean it, darling! Don't know what I'm saying. . . ."

She sat down beside him, bent over, her face in her hands. It was terrible for him, seeing her this way. He got up and walked from one side of the little room to the other.

He thought about what the white captain from Hattiesburg, Mississippi, had said. "Men, we have a job to do. Our outfit is just as damn important as any outfit in the United States Army, white or colored. And we're working towards complete integration. It's a long, hard pull, but I guarantee you every soldier will be treated equally and without discrimination. Remember, we're fighting for the dignity of the individual." Luke Robinson had looked at the tall, lanky captain with an arrogant smile.

Joe stopped in front of Cleo and made himself speak calmly. "Look, hon, it isn't like it used to be at all. Why can't you take my word for it? They're integrating colored soldiers now. And anyhow, what the hell's the use of getting all heated up about it? I *got* to go. That's all there is to it."

He sat down beside her again. He wanted fiercely to believe that things were really changing for his kind of people. Make it easier for him—make it much easier for him and Cleo, if they both believed that colored soldiers had a stake in fighting the war in Korea. Cleo wiped her eyes and blew her nose, and they changed the subject, talked about the baby; suppose it turned out to be a girl, what would her name be? A little after midnight he kissed her good night and walked back to the barracks.

The soldiers were marching in full field dress, with packs on their backs, duffle bags on their shoulders, and carbines and rifles. As they approached the big white ship, there was talking and joke-cracking and nervous laughter. They were the leading Negro outfit, immediately following the last of the white troops. Even at route step there was a certain uniform cadence in the sound of their feet striking the asphalt road as they moved forward under the midday sun, through a long funnel of people and palm trees and shrubbery. But Joe hadn't spotted Cleo yet, and he was getting sick from worry. Had anything happened?

Luke Robinson, beside him, was talking and laughing and grumbling. "Boy, I'm telling you, these peoples is tough on wheels. Say, Office Willie, what you reckon I read in your Harlem paper last night?" Office Willie was his nickname for Joe because Joe was the company clerk—a high-school graduate, two years in college, something special. "I read where some of your folks' leaders called on the President and demanded that colored soldiers be allowed to fight at the front instead of in quartermaster. Ain't that a damn shame?"

Joe's eyes shifted distractedly from the line of people to Luke, and back to the people again.

"Percy Johnson can have my uniform any day in the week," said Luke. "He want to fight so bad. Them damn Koreans ain't done me nothing. I ain't mad with a living soul."

Joe liked Luke Robinson, only he was so damn sensitive on the color question. Many times Joe had told him to take the chip off his shoulder and be somebody. But he had no time for Luke now. Seeing the ship plainly, and the white troops getting aboard, he felt a growing fear. Fear that maybe he had passed Cleo and they hadn't seen each other for looking so damn hard. Fear that he wouldn't get to see her at all—never-ever again. Maybe she was ill, with no way to let him know, too sick to move. He thought of what she had said last night, about little Joey. Maybe. . . .

And then he saw her, up ahead, waving at him, with the widest and prettiest and most confident smile anybody ever smiled. He was so damn glad he could hardly move his lips to smile or laugh or anything else.

She ran right up to him. "Hello, soldier boy, where you think you're going?"

"Damn," he said finally in as calm a voice as he could manage. "I thought for a while you had forgotten what day it was. Thought you had forgotten to come to my going-away party."

"Now, how do you sound?" She laughed at the funny look on his face and told him he looked cute with dark glasses on, needing a shave and with the pack on his back. She seemed so cheerful, he couldn't believe she was the same person who had completely broken down last night. He felt the tears rush out of his eyes and spill down his face.

She pretended not to notice and walked with him till they reached the last block. The women were not allowed to go any further. Looking at her, he wished somehow that she would cry, just a little bit anyhow. But she didn't cry at all. She reached up and kissed him quickly. "Good-bye, darling; take care of yourself. Little Joey and I will write every day, beginning this afternoon." And then she was gone.

The last of the white soldiers were boarding the beautiful white ship, and a band on board was playing "God Bless America." He felt a chill, like an electric current, pass across his slight shoulders, and he wasn't sure whether it was from "God Bless America" or from leaving Cleo behind. He hoped she could hear the music; maybe it would make her understand why Americans, no matter what their color, had to go and fight so many thousands of miles away from home.

They stopped in the middle of the block and stood waiting till the white regiment was all aboard. He wanted to look back for one last glimpse of Cleo, but he wouldn't let himself. Then they started again, marching toward the ship. And suddenly the band stopped playing "God Bless America" and jumped into another tune—"The Darktown Strutters' Ball. . . ."

He didn't want to believe his ears. He looked up at the ship and saw some of the white soldiers on deck waving and smiling at the Negro soldiers, yelling "Yeah, man!" and popping their fingers. A taste of gall crept up from his stomach into his mouth.

"Damn," he heard Luke say, "that's the kind of music I like." The husky soldier cut a little step. "I guess Mr. Charlie want us to jitterbug onto his pretty white boat. Equal treatment. . . . We ain't no soldiers; we're a bunch of damn clowns."

Joe felt an awful heat growing inside his collar. He hoped fiercely that Cleo was too far away to hear.

Luke grinned at him. "What's the matter, good kid? Mad about something? Damn—that's what I hate about you colored folks. Take that damn chip off your shoulder. They just trying to make you people feel at home. Don't you recognize the Negro national anthem when you hear it?"

Joe didn't answer. He just felt his anger mounting, and he wished he could walk right out of line and to hell with everything. But with "The Darktown Strutters' Ball" ringing in his ears, he put his head up, threw his shoulders back, and kept on marching towards the big white boat.

FOR DISCUSSION

1. Why do you think Killens chose the title "God Bless America"? Would "The Darktown Strutters' Ball" have been a better title?

2. Do you agree with Cleo that Black soldiers have nothing to fight for? How do you suppose the author would answer this question?

3. Why does Killens include the character Luke Robinson? Sometimes Luke seems to speak as if he were a white man. Why?

Negroes Have a Right to Fight Back

There is this scene in the movie *Elmer Gantry,* which was adapted from Sinclair Lewis's novel of the same title, in which this thug is slapping this prostitute around. At which point Burt Lancaster comes in, walks over to the thug, and says something like, "Hey, fellow, don't you know that hurts?" And smashes his fist magnificently up against the thug's head and generally kicks the thug around, just to emphasize the point.

It was a beautiful moment in the movie, and it crystallized my own attitude toward the merits (moral and practical) of nonviolence as a policy for Negroes. The perpetrators of violence must be made to know how it feels to be recipients of violence. How can they know unless we teach them?

I remember as a child on Virgin Street in Macon, Georgia, there was this boy who took delight in punching me, and one of his favorite sports was twisting my arm. Onlookers would try to prevail upon him: "Shame! Shame! The Lord is not going to bless you!" Which admonitions seemed to spur my adversary on and on.

One day I put two "alley apples" (pieces of brick) in my trousers' pockets and ventured forth. I was hardly out in the sun-washed streets before Bully-boy playfully accosted me. He immediately began his game of punching me in the stomach, laughing all the while. He was almost a foot taller than I, but I reached into my pockets and leaped up at both sides of his head with the alley apples. Bully-boy ran off. We later became great friends. We never could have become friends on the basis of him kicking my backside, and my counter-attack consisting solely of "Peace, brother!"

The one thing most friends and all enemies of the Afro-American have agreed upon is that we are ordained by nature and by God to be nonviolent. And so a new myth about the Negro is abroad throughout the land, to go with the old myths of laziness and rhythm and irresponsibility and sexual prowess. In the last third of the 20th century, when the disfranchised all over the earth are on the move, the world is being told that the good old U.S.A. has evolved a new type of *Homo sapiens,* the nonviolent Negro. The most disturbing aspect of this question is that many Negroes have bought this myth and are spreading it around.

One of the basic attributes of manhood (when we say manhood, we mean womanhood, selfhood) is the right of self-defense. In the psychological castration of the Negro, the denial of his right of self-defense has been one of the main instruments. Let me make one thing clear: I am not at the moment interested in the question of the so-called castration of the American male by American womanhood, or "Momism." White Mama is a victim too. Indeed, Madame Simone de Beauvoir in *The Second Sex* hit the bull's-eye when she made the analogy between the training of bourgeois girls and the training of American Negroes to know their place and to stay forever in it.

I grew up in Macon under a "separate-but-equal" public-school system. On our way to our wooden-frame school we black kids had to walk through a middle-class white neighborhood. One day in spring a white boy on the way home from his pretty brick school with his comrades said innocently enough, "Hey, nigger, what you learn in school today?" Friendly-like.

"I learned your mother was a pig," the sassy black boy answered, not in the spirit of nonviolence. We were seven to eleven years of age.

The black boy's buddies laughed angrily, uproariously. The white lad slapped the black boy's face, and that was how the "race riot" started. We fist-fought, we rock-battled, we used sticks and baseball bats and everything else that came to hand. Nobody won. The "race riot" just sort of petered out. We black kids went home with cut lips and bloody noses, but we went home proud and happy and got our backsides whipped for tearing our school clothes, and by the next morning we had almost forgotten it.

Just before noon next day our school ground swarmed with policemen. They strode into the classroom without so much as a "good morning" to the teachers and dragged kids out. They took those who had been in the "riot" and some who'd never even heard of it. The next move was to bring scared black mothers to the jailhouses to whip their children in order to "teach them they must not fight white children." Not a single white lad was arrested—naturally. And so they drove the lesson home. The black American must expect his person to be violated by the white man, but he must know that the white man's person is inviolable.

As an African-American, especially in the hospitable Southland, I concede that nonviolence is a legitimate tactic. It is practical and pragmatic; it has placed the question morally before the nation and the world. But the tendency is to take a tactic and build it into a way of life, to construct a whole new ideology and rhetoric around it. The danger is that all other means of struggle will be proscribed.

We black folk must never, tacitly or otherwise, surrender one single right guaranteed to any other American. The right of self-defense is the most basic of human rights, recognized by all people everywhere. It is certainly more important than the right to eat frankfurters while sitting down, or to get a black haircut in a white barbershop, or to get a night's lodging in Mrs. Murphy's flophouse, may the good Lord rest her soul. Indeed, it is more important than the right to vote. In many places in the South the Negro can't get to the polls without the right of self-defense.

A man's home is his castle, but a man's "castle" is really made of flesh and bones and heart and soul. One's castle is also one's wife and children, one's people, one's dignity. Invade this castle at your peril is the way the freedom script must read.

I was in Montgomery during the bus-protest movement. I was told on more than one occasion that most Negro men had stopped riding the buses long before the protest started because they could not stand to hear their women insulted by the brave bus drivers. Here the alternatives were sharp and clear: debasement, death, or tired feet. Black citizens of Montgomery did not have the right to be violent, by word or action, toward men who practiced every type of violence against them.

I also know that despite all the preaching about non-violence, the South is an armed camp. It always has been, ever since I can remember. The first time my wife, who is Brooklyn-born, went south with me, she was shocked to see so many guns in African-American homes. Of course, the white establishment has even vaster fire power, including the guns of the forces of law and order.

Yet, as I said before, nonviolence has the power of moral suasion,[1] which makes it possible to solicit help from many white and liberal summer soldiers, who would otherwise shrink rapidly from the cause. But moral suasion alone never brought about a revolution, for the simple reason that any power structure always constructs for itself a morality which is calculated to perpetuate itself forever. Ask Governor Wallace if the civil rights movement isn't the work of satanic forces. How many centuries of moral suasion would it have taken to convince the kindly Christian Southern slave masters that slavery was evil or to convince the Nazis at Auschwitz that morality was not on their side?

Before leading the Negro people of Birmingham into a demonstration in that city, the Rev. Martin Luther King was reported to have said, "If blood is shed, let it be our blood!" But our blood has always been the blood that was shed. And where is the morality that makes the white racist's blood more sacred than that of black children? I cannot believe that Dr. King meant these words, if indeed he ever uttered them. I can only believe that he got carried away by the dramatics of the moment. Dr. King is one of the men whom I hold in great esteem. We have been friends since 1957. But he loses me and millions of other black Americans when he calls upon us to love our abusers.

"Kick me and I will still love you! Spit on me and I will still love you!"

My daughter, who loves him dearly, heard him say words to this effect on the radio one day. She was in tears for her black hero. "Daddy! Daddy! What's the matter with Rev.

---

[1] SUASION: persuasion; influence.

King? What's the matter with Rev. King?"

I agree with Chuck and Barbara (my son and daughter). There is no dignity for me in allowing a man to spit on me with impunity. There is only sickness on the part of both of us, and it will beget an ever greater sickness. It degrades me and brutalizes him. If black folk were so sick as to love those who practice genocide against us, we would not deserve human consideration.

The advocates of nonviolence have not reckoned with the psychological needs of black America. There is in many Negroes a deep need to practice violence against their white tormentors. We black folk dearly loved the great Joe Louis, the heavyweight champion the white folk dubbed "The Brown Bomber." Each time he whipped another white man, black hearts overflowed with joy. Joe was strong wine for our much-abused egos.

I was at Yankee Stadium the night our champ knocked out Max Schmeling, the German fighter, in the first round. I saw black men who were strangers embrace each other, unashamedly, and weep for joy. And Joe was in the American tradition. Americans have always been men of violence, and proud of it.

We are a country born in violence. Malcolm X, the Black Nationalist leader who was murdered, knew this basic truth. He did not preach violence, but he did advocate self-defense. That is one of the reasons he had such tremendous attraction for the people of the ghetto. What I am saying is that the so-called race riots are healthier (from the point of view of the ghetto people) than the internecine[2] gang warfare which was the vogue in the ghettos a few years ago, when black teen-agers killed each other or killed equally helpless Puerto Ricans, as was often the case in New York City. Historically in the black ghettos the helpless and hopeless have practiced violence on each other. Stand around the emergency entrance at Harlem Hospital of a Saturday night and check the business in black blood drawn

[2] INTERNECINE (ĭn·tər·nĕs'ēn): mutually deadly.

by black hands that comes in every weekend.

It is time for Americans (black and white) to stop hood-winking themselves. Nonviolence is a tactic, but it must never be a way of life for the black American. Just because I love myself, the black *Me*, why do white Americans (especially liberals) think it means I have to hate the white American *You?* We black and white folk in the U.S.A. have to settle many things between us before the matter of love can be discussed. For one thing, if you practice violence against me, I mean to give it back to you in kind.

Most black folk believe in the kind of nonviolence that keeps everybody nonviolent. For example: In a certain cotton county in the heart of Dixieland, black folk, most of them sharecroppers, asserted their right to vote and were driven from the land. For several years they lived in tents, and of a Saturday evening white pranksters had a playful way of driving out to Tent City and shooting into it. A couple of campers were injured, including a pregnant woman. Complaints to the authorities got no results at all. So one Saturday evening when the pranksters turned up, just to have a little sport, the campers (lacking a sense of humor) returned the fire. A young relative of the sheriff got his arm shattered. The sheriff got out there in a hurry and found rifles shining out of every tent. He sent for the Negro leader.

"Tell them to give up them rifles, boy. I can't protect 'em less'n they surrender up them rifles."

Whereupon the 35-year-old "boy" said, "We figured you was kind of busy, Sheriff. We thought we'd give you a helping hand and protect our own selves." There was no more racial violence in the county for a long time.

Let us speak plainly to each other. Your black brother is spoiling for a fight in affirmation of his selfhood. This is the meaning of Watts and Harlem and Bedford-Stuyvesant. It seems to me, you folk who abhor violence, you are barking up the wrong tree when you come to black folk and call on them to be nonviolent. Go to the attackers. Go to the ones who start the fire, not to the firefighters. Insist that your Government place the same premium on black life as it does on white. As far as I can ascertain, no white American has ever been condemned to death by the courts for taking a black life.

The Deacons of Defense, the Negro self-defense organization that started in Louisiana not long ago, is going to mushroom and increasingly become a necessary appendage to the civil rights movement. This should be welcomed by everyone who is sincere about the "Negro revolution." It accomplishes three things simultaneously. It makes certain that the Government will play the role of the fire department, the pacifier. Second: The actual physical presence of the Deacons (or any similar group) will go a long way in staying the hands of the violence makers. Third: It further affirms the black Americans' determination to exercise every right enjoyed by all other Americans.

Otherwise we're in for longer and hotter summers. There are all kinds among us black folks. Gentle ones and angry ones, forgiving and vindictive, and every single one is determined to be free. Julian Bond, poet, SNCC[3] leader, and duly elected member of the Georgia legislature (his seat was denied him because of his pronouncements on Vietnam), summed up the situation when he wrote:

> Look at that gal shake that thing.
> We cannot all be Martin Luther King.

I believe he meant, among other things, that whites cannot expect Negroes to be different—that is, more saintly than whites are—and that most black folk are in no mood to give up the right to defend themselves.

[3] SNCC: Student Nonviolent Coordinating Committee, founded in 1960 by southern Black college students to guide desegregation activities.

FOR DISCUSSION

1. At what times and under what conditions does Killens think that violence is necessary and morally acceptable? Do you agree?

2. Killens says that "One of the basic attributes of manhood . . . is the right of self-defense." What does Killens mean by the word *manhood?* What is your own definition of the word? Is self-defense a necessary part of manhood? Why or why not?

3. Killens asks: "How many centuries of moral suasion would it have taken to convince the kindly Christian Southern slave masters that slavery was evil . . . ?" What does Killens mean by "moral suasion"? Do you think that moral suasion can ever overcome evil?

4. Killens says that "Americans have always been men of violence, and proud of it." Drawing on your experience and reading, do you agree with this statement?

James Baldwin

b. 1924

One of America's foremost novelists and essayists, James Baldwin first began writing in high school, where he was editor of his school magazine. After graduation, he worked as an office boy, a factory worker, a dishwasher, and a waiter while he wrote in his spare time. In 1948 Baldwin won a Eugene Saxton Fellowship, an award given to promising young writers, and moved to Europe to begin a full-time writing career; he remained in Europe until 1956. During this period Baldwin published his first novel, Go Tell It On the Mountain, *and his first book of essays,* Notes of a Native Son. *His next two books of essays,* Nobody Knows My Name *and* The Fire Next Time, *established his reputation as a writer and brought him recognition as an articulate spokesman for Black protest. Baldwin portrays the Black man's search for identity in America and repeatedly insists that the real victim of bigotry is the white man who hides his weakness under his myth of superiority.*

The Rockpile

Across the street from their house, in an empty lot between two houses, stood the rockpile. It was a strange place to find a mass of natural rock jutting out of the ground; and

97

someone, probably Aunt Florence, had once told them that
the rock was there and could not be taken away because
without it the subway cars underground would fly apart,
killing all the people. This, touching on some natural mys-
tery concerning the surface and the center of the earth, was
far too intriguing an explanation to be challenged, and it
invested the rockpile, moreover, with such mysterious importance that Roy felt it to be his right, not to say his duty,
to play there.

Other boys were to be seen there each afternoon after
school and all day Saturday and Sunday. They fought on
the rockpile. Sure-footed, dangerous, and reckless, they
rushed each other and grappled on the heights, sometimes
disappearing down the other side in a confusion of dust and
screams and upended, flying feet. "It's a wonder they don't
kill themselves," their mother said, watching sometimes
from the fire escape. "You children stay away from there,
you hear me?" Though she said "children," she was looking at Roy, where he sat beside John on the fire escape.
"The good Lord knows," she continued, "I don't want you
to come home bleeding like a hog every day the Lord
sends." Roy shifted impatiently and continued to stare at
the street, as though in this gazing he might somehow ac-
quire wings. John said nothing. He had not really been spoken to: he was afraid of the rockpile and of the boys who
played there.

Each Saturday morning John and Roy sat on the fire
escape and watched the forbidden street below. Sometimes
their mother sat in the room behind them, sewing, or dress-
ing their younger sister, or nursing the baby, Paul. The sun
fell across them and across the fire escape with a high,
benevolent indifference; below them, men and women,
and boys and girls, sinners all, loitered; sometimes one of
the church members passed and saw them and waved.
Then, for the moment that they waved decorously back,
they were intimidated. They watched the saint, man or
woman, until he or she had disappeared from sight. The
passage of one of the redeemed made them consider, however vacantly, the wickedness of the street, their own latent
wickedness in sitting where they sat, and made them think

of their father, who came home early on Saturdays and who would soon be turning this corner and entering the dark hall below them.

But until he came to end their freedom, they sat, watching and longing above the street. At the end of the street nearest their house was the bridge which spanned the Harlem River and led to a city called the Bronx, which was where Aunt Florence lived. Nevertheless, when they saw her coming, she did not come from the bridge, but from the opposite end of the street. This weakly, to their minds, she explained by saying that she had taken the subway, not wishing to walk, and that, besides, she did not live in *that* section of the Bronx. Knowing that the Bronx was across the river, they did not believe this story ever, but, adopting toward her their father's attitude, assumed that she had just left some sinful place which she dared not name, as, for example, a movie palace.

In the summertime boys swam in the river, diving off the wooden dock or wading in from the garbage-heavy bank. Once a boy, whose name was Richard, drowned in the river. His mother had not known where he was; she had even come to their house, to ask if he was there. Then, in the evening, at six o'clock, they had heard from the street a woman screaming and wailing, and they ran to the windows and looked out. Down the street came the woman, Richard's mother, screaming, her face raised to the sky and tears running down her face. A woman walked beside her, trying to make her quiet and trying to hold her up. Behind them walked a man, Richard's father, with Richard's body in his arms. There were two white policemen walking in the gutter, who did not seem to know what should be done. Richard's father and Richard were wet, and Richard's body lay across his father's arms like a cotton baby. The woman's screaming filled all the street; cars slowed down and the people in the cars stared; people opened their windows and looked out and came rushing out of doors to stand in the gutter, watching. Then the small procession disappeared within the house which stood beside the rockpile. Then, *"Lord, Lord, Lord!"* cried Elizabeth, their mother, and slammed the window down.

One Saturday, an hour before his father would be coming home, Roy was wounded on the rockpile and brought screaming upstairs. He and John had been sitting on the fire escape, and their mother had gone into the kitchen to sip tea with Sister McCandless. By and by Roy became bored and sat beside John in restless silence; and John began drawing into his schoolbook a newspaper advertisement which featured a new electric locomotive. Some friends of Roy passed beneath the fire escape and called him. Roy began to fidget, yelling down to them through the bars. Then a silence fell. John looked up. Roy stood looking at him.

"I'm going downstairs," he said.

"You better stay where you is, boy. You know mama don't want you going downstairs."

"I be right *back*. She won't even know I'm gone, less you run and tell her."

"I ain't *got* to tell her. What's going to stop her from coming in here and looking out the window?"

"She's talking," Roy said. He started into the house.

"But daddy's going to be home soon!"

"I be back before *that*. What you all the time got to be so *scared* for?" He was already in the house, and he now turned, leaning on the windowsill, to swear impatiently, "I be back in *five* minutes."

John watched him sourly as he carefully unlocked the door and disappeared. In a moment he saw him on the sidewalk with his friends. He did not dare to go and tell his mother that Roy had left the fire escape, because he had practically promised not to. He started to shout, *Remember, you said five minutes!* but one of Roy's friends was looking up at the fire escape. John looked down at his schoolbook: he became engrossed again in the problem of the locomotive.

When he looked up again, he did not know how much time had passed, but now there was a gang fight on the rockpile. Dozens of boys fought each other in the harsh sun: clambering up the rocks and battling hand to hand, scuffed shoes sliding on the slippery rock, filling the bright air with curses and jubilant cries. They filled the air, too, with flying weapons: stones, sticks, tin cans, garbage, whatever could be picked up and thrown. John watched in a kind of absent amazement—until he remembered that Roy was still downstairs and that he was one of the boys on the rockpile. Then he was afraid; he could not see his brother among the figures in the sun; and he stood up, leaning over the fire-escape railing. Then Roy appeared from the other side of the rocks; John saw that his shirt was torn; he was laughing. He moved until he stood at the very top of the rockpile. Then, something, an empty tin can, flew out of the air and hit him on the forehead, just above the eye. Immediately, one side of Roy's face ran with blood; he fell and rolled on his face down the rocks. Then for a moment there was no movement at all, no sound; the sun, arrested, lay on the street and the sidewalk and the arrested boys. Then some-one screamed or shouted; boys began to run away, down the street, toward the bridge. The figure on the ground, having caught its breath and felt its own blood, began to shout. John cried, "Mama! Mama!" and ran inside.

"Don't fret, don't fret," panted Sister McCandless as they rushed down the dark, narrow, swaying stairs, "don't fret. Ain't a boy been born don't get his knocks every now and again. *Lord!*" They hurried into the sun. A man had picked Roy up and now walked slowly toward them. One or two boys sat silent on their stoops; at either end of the street there was a group of boys watching. "He ain't hurt bad," the man said. "Wouldn't be making this kind of noise if he was hurt real bad."

Elizabeth, trembling, reached out to take Roy, but Sister McCandless, bigger, calmer, took him from the man and threw him over her shoulder as she once might have han-dled a sack of cotton. "God bless you," she said to the man, "God bless you, son." Roy was still screaming. Elizabeth stood behind Sister McCandless to stare at his bloody face.

"It's just a flesh wound," the man kept saying, "just broke the skin, that's all." They were moving across the sidewalk, toward the house. John, not now afraid of the staring boys, looked toward the corner to see if his father was yet in sight.

Upstairs, they hushed Roy's crying. They bathed the blood away, to find, just above the left eyebrow, the jagged, superficial scar. "Lord, have mercy," murmured Elizabeth, "another inch and it would've been his eye." And she looked with apprehension toward the clock. "Ain't it the truth," said Sister McCandless, busy with bandages and iodine.

"When did he go downstairs?" his mother asked at last.

Sister McCandless now sat fanning herself in the easy chair, at the head of the sofa where Roy lay, bound and silent. She paused for a moment to look sharply at John. John stood near the window, holding the newspaper advertisement and the drawing he had done.

"We was sitting on the fire escape," he said. "Some boys he knew called him."

"When?"

"He said he'd be back in five minutes."

"Why didn't you tell me he was downstairs?"

He looked at his hands, clasping his notebook, and did not answer.

"Boy," said Sister McCandless, "you hear your mother a-talking to you?"

He looked at his mother. He repeated: "He said he'd be back in five minutes."

"He said he'd be back in five minutes," said Sister McCandless with scorn, "don't look to me like that's no right answer. You's the man of the house, you supposed to look after your baby brothers and sisters—you ain't supposed to let them run off and get half-killed. But I expect," she added, rising from the chair, dropping the cardboard fan, "your daddy'll make you tell the truth. Your ma's way too soft with you."

He did not look at her, but at the fan where it lay in the dark red, depressed seat where she had been. The fan advertised a pomade for the hair and showed a brown woman and her baby, both with glistening hair, smiling happily at each other.

"Honey," said Sister McCandless, "I got to be moving along. Maybe I drop in later tonight. I don't reckon you going to be at Tarry Service tonight?"

Tarry Service was the prayer meeting held every Saturday night at church to strengthen believers and prepare the church for the coming of the Holy Ghost on Sunday.

"I don't reckon," said Elizabeth. She stood up; she and Sister McCandless kissed each other on the cheek. "But you be sure to remember me in your prayers."

"I surely will do that." She paused, with her hand on the doorknob, and looked down at Roy and laughed. "Poor little man," she said, "reckon he'll be content to sit on the fire escape *now*."

Elizabeth laughed with her. "It sure ought to be a lesson to him. You don't reckon," she asked nervously, still smiling, "he going to keep that scar, do you?"

"Lord, no," said Sister McCandless, "Ain't nothing but a scratch. I declare, Sister Grimes, you worse than a child. Another couple of weeks and you won't be able to *see* no scar. No, you go on about your housework, honey, and thank the Lord it weren't no worse." She opened the door; they heard the sound of feet on the stairs. "I expect that's the Reverend," said Sister McCandless, placidly; "I *bet* he going to raise cain."

"Maybe it's Florence," Elizabeth said. "Sometimes she get here about this time." They stood in the doorway, staring, while the steps reached the landing below and began again climbing to their floor. "No," said Elizabeth then, "that ain't her walk. That's Gabriel."

"Well, I'll just go on," said Sister McCandless, "and kind of prepare his mind." She pressed Elizabeth's hand as she spoke and started into the hall, leaving the door behind her slightly ajar. Elizabeth turned slowly back into the room. Roy did not open his eyes, or move; but she knew that he was not sleeping; he wished to delay until the last possible moment any contact with his father. John put his newspaper and his notebook on the table and stood, leaning on the table, staring at her.

"It wasn't my fault," he said. "I couldn't stop him from going downstairs."

"No," she said, "you ain't got nothing to worry about. You just tell your daddy the truth."

He looked directly at her, and she turned to the window,

staring into the street. What was Sister McCandless saying? Then from her bedroom she heard Delilah's thin wail, and she turned, frowning, looking toward the bedroom and toward the still-open door. She knew that John was watching her. Delilah continued to wail; she thought, angrily, *Now that girl's getting too big for that*, but she feared that Delilah would awaken Paul, and she hurried into the bedroom. She tried to soothe Delilah back to sleep. Then she heard the front door open and close—too loud; Delilah raised her voice; with an exasperated sigh Elizabeth picked the child up. Her child and Gabriel's, her children and Gabriel's: Roy, Delilah, Paul. Only John was nameless and a stranger, living, unalterable testimony to his mother's days in sin.

"What happened?" Gabriel demanded. He stood, enormous, in the center of the room, his black lunchbox dangling from his hand, staring at the sofa where Roy lay. John stood just before him, it seemed to her astonished vision just below him, beneath his fist, his heavy shoe. The child stared at the man in fascination and terror—when a girl down home she had seen rabbits stand so paralyzed before the barking dog. She hurried past Gabriel to the sofa, feeling the weight of Delilah in her arms like the weight of a shield, and stood over Roy, saying:

"Now, ain't a thing to get upset about, Gabriel. This boy sneaked downstairs while I had my back turned and got hisself hurt a little. He's alright now."

Roy, as though in confirmation, now opened his eyes and looked gravely at his father. Gabriel dropped his lunchbox with a clatter and knelt by the sofa.

"How you feel, son? Tell your daddy what happened?"

Roy opened his mouth to speak and then, relapsing into panic, began to cry. His father held him by the shoulder.

"You don't want to cry. You's daddy's little man. Tell your daddy what happened."

"He went downstairs," said Elizabeth, "where he didn't have no business to be, and got to fighting with them bad boys playing on that rockpile. That's what happened, and it's a mercy it weren't nothing worse."

He looked up at her. "Can't you let this boy answer me for hisself?"

Ignoring this, she went on, more gently: "He got cut on the forehead, but it ain't nothing to worry about."

"You call a doctor? How you know it ain't nothing to worry about?"

"Is you got money to be throwing away on doctors? No, I ain't called no doctor. Ain't nothing wrong with my eyes that I can't tell whether he's hurt bad or not. He got a fright more'n anything else, and you ought to pray God it teaches him a lesson."

"You got a lot to say *now*," he said, "but I'll have *me* something to say in a minute. I'll be wanting to know when all this happened, what you was doing with your eyes *then*." He turned back to Roy, who had lain quietly sobbing, eyes wide open and body held rigid: and who now, at his father's touch, remembered the height, the sharp, sliding rock beneath his feet, the sun, the explosion of the sun, his plunge into darkness and his salty blood; and recoiled, beginning to scream, as his father touched his forehead. "Hold still, hold still," crooned his father, shaking; "hold still. Don't cry. Daddy ain't going to hurt you; he just wants to see this bandage, see what they've done to his little man." But Roy continued to scream and would not be still, and Gabriel dared not lift the bandage for fear of hurting him more. And he looked at Elizabeth in fury: "Can't you put that child down and help me with this boy? John, take your baby sister from your mother—don't look like neither of you got good sense."

John took Delilah and sat down with her in the easy chair. His mother bent over Roy and held him still, while his father, carefully—but still Roy screamed—lifted the bandage and stared at the wound. Roy's sobs began to lessen. Gabriel readjusted the bandage. "You see," said Elizabeth, finally, "he ain't nowhere near dead."

"It sure ain't your fault that he ain't dead." He and Elizabeth considered each other for a moment in silence. "He came mightly close to losing an eye. Course, his eyes ain't as big as your'n, so I reckon you don't think it matters so much." At this her face hardened; he smiled. "Lord, have mercy," he said, "you think you ever going to learn to do right? Where was you when all this happened? Who let him go downstairs?"

"Ain't nobody let him go downstairs; he just went. He got a head just like his father; it got to be broken before it'll bow. I was in the kitchen."

"Where was Johnnie?"

"He was in here."

"Where?"

"He was on the fire escape."

"Didn't he know Roy was downstairs?"

"I reckon."

"What you mean, you reckon? He ain't got your big eyes for nothing, does he?" He looked over at John. "Boy, you see your brother go downstairs?"

"Gabriel, ain't no sense in trying to blame Johnnie. You know right well if you have trouble making Roy behave, he ain't going to listen to his brother. He don't hardly listen to me."

"How come you didn't tell your mother Roy was downstairs?"

John said nothing, staring at the blanket which covered Delilah.

"Boy, you hear me? You want me to take a strap to you?"

"No, you ain't," she said. "You ain't going to take no strap to this boy, not today you ain't. Ain't a soul to blame for Roy's lying up there now but you—you because you done spoiled him so that he thinks he can do just anything and get away with it. I'm here to tell you that ain't no way to raise no child. You don't pray to the Lord to help you do better than you been doing, you going to live to shed bitter tears that the Lord didn't take his soul today." And she was trembling. She moved, unseeing, toward John and took Delilah from his arms. She looked back at Gabriel, who had risen, who stood near the sofa, staring at her. And she found in his face not fury alone, which would not have surprised her; but hatred so deep as to become insupportable in its lack of personality. His eyes were struck alive, unmoving, blind with malevolence—she felt, like the pull of the earth at her feet, his longing to witness her perdition. Again, as though it might be propitiation,[1] she moved the child in her arms. And at this his eyes changed; he looked at Elizabeth, the mother of his children, the helpmeet given by the Lord. Then her eyes clouded; she moved to leave the room; her foot struck the lunchbox lying on the floor.

"John," she said, "pick up your father's lunchbox like a good boy."

She heard, behind her, his scrambling movement as he left the easy chair, the scrape and jangle of the lunchbox as he picked it up, bending his dark head near the toe of his father's heavy shoe.

[1] PROPITIATION (prō·pĭsh·ē·ā′shən): here, appeasement, in the sense of doing something to ward off the ill will or anger of some higher being.

FOR DISCUSSION

1. Describe the rockpile and explain what it represents. At the beginning of the story, the author describes a parent's response to the drowning of her son, a boy named Richard. What is the purpose of this long description?

2. What kind of person is Gabriel? Explain the effect he has on his family.

William Melvin Kelley

b. 1937

When only twenty-five years old, William Melvin Kelley published his first novel, A Different Drummer. *Highly acclaimed by critics, this novel established the theme which Kelley develops in his later works, "the plight of Negroes, as individual human beings, in America." Born in New York City, Kelley attended Harvard University, where he studied under the direction of Archibald MacLeish and John Hawkes. His writing efforts have confirmed Kelley as one of America's most promising young authors; among other significant awards, he has received the Dana Reed Literary Prize. "A Good Long Sidewalk" is taken from* Dancers on the Shore, *a collection of his short stories published in 1964. A* Drop of Patience *and* Dem *are other notable works by this talented author.*

A Good Long Sidewalk

It seemed much colder with his hair cut short, his neck shaved clean. Carlyle trudged flat-footed, planting his feet firmly so as not to slip, up the middle of the carless street, through the shadows cast by the snow-clogged trees. He wished he could go home, take off his wet shoes, listen to records, and read the paper that each night his father carried home tucked under his arm. He knew too that the later it got, the angrier his father would be; his father liked to eat as soon as he came home. Besides, his father would want him or his little brother to clear their own driveway, and Carlyle had not asked to take the shovel. He decided then, walking along the rutted street, he would not waste his time with small jobs; he would look for a long snow-banked walk of a house set way back from the street.

This is what he finally found, down a solitary side street lit faintly by a single street lamp at the middle of the block; the house, set back on a short hill that surely, in the spring and summer, would be a thick lawn, perhaps bordered with flowers. Snow clung to the empty, blackened branches of a hedge concealing a grotesque iron fence. The house too was grotesque, painted gray, its gables hung with dagger-like icicles.

He hesitated a moment, looking up at the house; there did not seem to be any light burning, and he did not want to wade twenty or thirty feet through shin-deep snow only to find no one at home. Going farther on up the sidewalk, he found a lighted window down the side near the back, and he returned to the gate and started up the drifted walk.

The porch was wood and clunked hollow when he stamped the snow from his feet. He climbed the steps gingerly and peered at the names on the doorbell. If there was a man's name, he still might not find work—women living alone or old couples more usually needed someone to clean snow. There was a woman's name—Elizabeth Reuben—and a man's too, but his, which was typed, had been recently crossed out. Carlyle rang the bell.

No longer walking, his feet got cold very quickly and when, after what seemed a long while, the door opened—and then only a crack—he was hopping from one foot to the other.

"Yes? What is it?" He could see a nose and one eye, could hear a woman's voice.

"Miz Reuben?" He slurred the *miss* or *missus* so as not to insult her either way.

"Yes."

"Would you like to have your walk shoveled?" He moved closer and spoke to the nose and eye.

There was a pause while she looked him over, up and down, and inspected the shovel he held in his hand. "No. I'm sorry. I don't think so."

"Well, uh...." There was nothing else to say. He thanked her and turned away.

"Wait!" It sounded almost like a scream. And then softer: "Young man, wait."

He turned back and found the door swung wide. The nose and eye had grown to a small, plumpish, white woman of about forty in a pale blue wool dress. She was not exactly what he would have called pretty, but she was by no means a hag. She was just uninteresting looking. Her hair was a dull brown combed into a style that did her no good; her eyes were flat and gray like cardboard. "On second thought, young man, I think it would be nice to have my walk cleaned off. I'm expecting some visitors and it will make it easier for them ... to find me." She smiled at him. "But come inside; you must be frozen solid walking around in all this snow and cold."

"That's all right, ma'am. I'll start right away." He took a step back and lifted his shovel.

"You do as I say and come in the house this very moment." She was still smiling, but there was enough of a mother's tone in her voice to make him walk past her through the door, which she closed behind him. "Rest your coat and shovel there and follow me. I'm taking you into the kitchen to put something warm into your stomach."

He did as she ordered and walked behind her down the hall, lit by a low-watt bulb in a yellowing shade.

The first thing he noticed was that the kitchen smelled of leaking gas. There was a huge pile of rags and bits of cloth on the table in the center of the room. There were more rags on the windowsill and stuffed at the bottom of the back door.

She saw him looking at them. "It's an old house. It gets very drafty." She smiled nervously, wringing her hands. "Now, are you old enough to drink coffee? Or would you rather have hot chocolate?"

He had remained on his feet. She bustled to the table and swept the rags onto the floor with her arm. "Sit down, please." He did. "Now, what would you rather have?"

"Hot chocolate, please."

"Hot chocolate? Good. That's better for you." She headed toward the stove, almost running; it was big and old-fashioned with a shelf for salt and pepper above the burners. "What's your name, dear?"

"Carlyle, ma'am. Carlyle Bedlow."

"Carlyle? Did you know you were named after a famous man?"

"No, ma'am. I was just named after my father. His name's—"

She was laughing, shrilly, unhappily. He had said something funny but did not know what it was. It made him uneasy.

"What, dear? You started to say something. I interrupted you."

"Nothing, ma'am." He was wondering now what he had said, and why she was being so nice, giving him hot chocolate. Maybe she was giving him the hot chocolate so she could talk to him about things he did not understand and laugh at his ignorance. It was just like the men in the barbershop said: Most of a colored man's trouble began with white people. They were always laughing and making fun of Negroes. . . .

"Do you like your hot chocolate sweet, Carlyle? I can put some sugar in it for you." Behind her voice he could hear the milk sizzling around the edges of the saucepan, could hear the gas feeding the flame.

"Yes, ma'am. I like it sweet."

The milk sizzled louder still as she poured it across the hot sides into his cup. She brought it and sat across from him on the edge of her chair, waiting for him to taste it. He did so and found it good; with his mind's eye, he followed it down his throat and into his stomach.

"Is it good?" Her gray eyes darted across his face.

"Yes, ma'am."

She smiled and seemed pleased. That puzzled him. If she had him in to laugh at him, why was she so anxious to get him warm, why did she want him to like the hot chocolate? There had to be some other reason, but just then the chocolate was too good to think about it. He took a big swallow.

"Well now, let's get down to business. I've never had to hire anybody to do this before. I used to do it myself when I was younger and . . . then . . . there was a man here who'd do it for me . . . but he's not here any more." She trailed off, caught herself. "How much do you usually get for a stoop and a walk that long?" She smiled at him again. It was a fleeting smile which warmed only the corners of her mouth and left her eyes sad. "I've been very nice to you. I should think you'd charge me less than usual."

So that was it! She wanted him to do her walk for practically nothing! White people were always trying to cheat Negroes. He had heard his father say that, cursing the Jews in Harlem. He just stared at her, hating her.

She waited an instant for him to answer, then started to figure out loud. "Well, let's see. That's a long walk and there's the sidewalk and the stoop and the steps and it's very cold and I probably can't get anyone else. . . . It's a question of too little supply and a great deal of demand." She was talking above him again. "I'd say I'd be getting off well if I gave you five dollars." She stopped and looked across at him, helplessly. "Does that sound fair? I really don't know."

He continued to stare, but now because he could hardly believe what she said. At the most, he would have charged only three dollars, and had expected her to offer one.

She filled in the silence. "Yes, five. That sounds right."

He finished his chocolate with a gulp. "But, ma'am, I wouldn't-a charged you but three. Really!"

"Three? That doesn't sound like enough." She bolted from the table and advanced on him. "Well, I'll give you the extra two for being honest. Perhaps you can come back and do something else for me." She swooped on him, hugged and kissed him. The kiss left a wet, cold spot on his cheek. He lurched away, surprised, knocking the cup and saucer from the table. The saucer broke in two; the cup bounced, rolled, lopsided and crazy, under the table.

"No, ma'am." He jumped to his feet. "I'm sorry, ma'am."

"That's all right. It's all right. I'm sor—That's all right about the saucer." She scrambled to her knees and began to pick up the pieces and the cup. Once she had them in her lap, she sat, staring away at nothing, shaking her head.

Now he knew for certain what she was up to; he remembered what Garland had said: When you find some white woman being nicer than she ought to be, then watch out! She wanted to make time with him. He started from the kitchen. Maybe he could leave before it was too late.

"Wait, young man." She stood up. "I'll pay you now, and you won't have to come inside when you're through." She pushed by him and hurried down the shadowy hallway. He followed her as before, but kept his distance.

Her purse was hanging on a peg on the coatrack, next to his own jacket. She took them both down, handed him his jacket, averting her eyes, and fumbled in her purse, produced a wallet, unzipped it, pulled out a bill, and handed it to him.

"But it's a five, ma'am." He could not understand why she wanted to pay him that much now that he was not going to make time with her.

She looked at him for the first time, her eyes wet. "I told you I'd pay you five, didn't I?"

"Yes, ma'am."

"All right. Do a good job. And remember, don't come back."

"Yes, ma'am."

"You let yourself out." She started to the back of the house even before he had finished buttoning his jacket. By the time he opened the door, she was far down the hall, and as he closed it behind him and stepped into the dark, twinkling cold, he could hear her in the kitchen. She was tearing rags.

The next evening the white woman was in the newspaper. A boy trying to deliver a package had found her in the gas-filled kitchen, slumped over a table piled high with rags. Carlyle's father, who saw it first, mentioned it at dinner. "Had a suicide a couple blocks from here." He told who and where.

Carlyle sat staring at his plate.

His father went on: "White folks! Man, if they had to be colored for a day, they'd all kill they-selves. We wouldn't have no race problem then. White folks don't know what hard life is. What's wrong, Junior?"

"She was a nice lady."

His parents and his little brother looked at him.

"You know her, Junior?" His mother put down her fork.

"She was a nice lady, mama. I shoveled her walk yesterday. She give me five dollars."

"Oh, Junior." His mother sighed.

"Five dollars?" His father leaned forward. "Crazy, huh?"

"Have some respect!" His mother turned on his father angrily.

Carlyle looked at his mother. "Are white people all bad? There's some good ones, ain't there, mama?"

"Of course, Junior." His mother smiled. "What made you think—"

"Sure, there is, Junior." His father was smiling too. "The dead ones is good."

FOR DISCUSSION

1. Why do you think "Miz" Reuben acted so nicely to Carlyle? Why was he uncomfortable in her presence?

2. Are you surprised to learn that Miz Reuben committed suicide? Do you think Carlyle agrees with his father about the white woman's death or about white people generally?

Junius Edwards

b. 1929

---

*A native of Louisiana, Junius Edwards was graduated from
the University of Oslo in Norway. In 1958 he was awarded
the Writer's Digest Award, and in 1959 he won a Eugene
Saxton Fellowship. His novel* If We Must Die *has firmly
established Mr. Edwards' reputation as a writer. At present,
the author lives in Westchester County with his wife and
four children and directs an advertising agency in New
York City.*

Mother Dear and Daddy

They came in the night while we slept. We knew they were
coming, but not when, and we expected to see them when
they did. We never thought that they would come at night.
When we got up, well, when John, my brother, got up (he
was always getting up early), when he got up, he looked out
of the window and ran and jumped back in bed and shook
me and called my name.

"Jim, Jim, they here. They here already. Wake up, Jim.
They—"

"Hey, quit shaking me. I been woke long time."

"They here," he ran to the window. "Come on look."

He didn't have to tell me "come on look," because I was
at the window when he got there, almost, anyway. They

115

had come, all right; we could see the cars parked in the yard, like big cats crouching, backs hunched, ready to attack.

"I'll go tell Mary, then," John said, and bolted out of the room as fast as you could blow out a coal oil lamp.

While he was out telling our three sisters, I stood there at the window and counted the cars. There were five in all, besides our car, and they were all black and shiny as my plate whenever I got through eating red beans and rice. Our car sat over there by itself, dusty and dirty as one of those bums that come by all the time wanting a meal.

I stood there, leaning on the windowsill, with my right foot on top of my left foot, scratching my left foot with my toes and looking at our car. I could feel my eyes burning, burning, and the tears coming and washing the burns, and me sucking my tongue because of the burning and trying not to make a sound. My body went cold, and inside it I could feel something surging up, not like being sick; this surging came up my whole body, my arms, too, and ended with my eyes burning. I fought to hold it back, keep it buried. Even when I was alone, I always fought it, always won and kept it down, even at times when it was sudden and fast and got to my eyes and burned like hot needles behind my eyelids, hot needles with legs running around trying to get past my eyelids and spill out on my cheeks; even then I kept it down.

I had fought it for two weeks, and I was good at it and getting better. Maybe I was good at it because of that first day. I had not fought it then. I had let it come, right in front of Aunt Mabel, I let it come, not trying to stop it, control it; I let it come.

"What we going to do?" I asked Aunt Mabel, after it had come, had shaken me and left me as empty as an unfilled grave. "What we going to do, Aunt Mabel?"

"Lord knows, son. Lord knows," Aunt Mabel said, sitting in her rocker, moving slow, back and forth, looking down at me, on my knees, my arms resting on her huge right thigh and my head turned up to her, watching that round face, her lips tight now, her head shaking side to side, and her eyes

clouded, and me not understanding her answer, but thinking I should and not daring to ask again and feeling the
question pounding my brain: What we going to do? What
we going to do?

"The Lord giveth and the Lord taketh away."

But, what we going to do? I could not understand Aunt
Mabel. I did not know what her mumbling about The Lord
had to do with this. All I knew was she had just told me
Mother Dear and Daddy were dead. Mother Dear and
Daddy were dead. Mother Dear and Daddy would not come
back. Mother Dear and Daddy wouldn't take us home again.
What we going to do?

"I want to go home. I want to go home," I screamed and
got to my feet and ran to the door, realizing it was Aunt
Mabel calling my name. I ran out to the yard where John
and our sisters played, and right past them. I did not feel
my feet move; I did not feel I owned a body. I wanted to
get home. And hearing Aunt Mabel call my name, seeing
houses, cars, people, trees, like one big thing made of
windows, walls, wheels, heads, branches, arms and legs,
and behind that one big thing, our house, with our car out
front, and our yard and our tree, and then the big thing was
gone and I was at our house, running up the steps across the
porch, as fast as I could, straight to the screened door,
wham! and I lay on my back on the porch looking up at the
screen, at the imprints made in it by my head and hands
and my right knee. I got right up and started banging on the
door, trying to twist the knob.

"Mother Dear! Daddy! Mother Dear! Daddy!" I called as
loud as I could and kept banging on the door. Then I ran
to the back door and called again and banged and kicked
the door. They did not come.

They would not come.

"Mother Dear! Daddy! It's me. Let me in. Open the
door!"

They would not come.

I ran to the front, out to the street and turned and looked
up to their room and saw the shades were drawn just as
they were drawn when Mother Dear and Daddy took us

over to Aunt Mabel's house to stay for the weekend while they went away fishing with Cousin Bob.

I cupped my hands up to my mouth.

"Mother Dear. Daddy. Mother Dear! Daddy!"

I called, and called again, and all the while I kept my eyes glued on that window, waiting. Any moment now, any second now, now, *now*, waited to see that white shade zoom up and then the window, and then Mother Dear and Daddy, both together, lean out, smiling, laughing, waving, calling my name, now, now, *now*.

They did not come.

They would not come. The shade stood still, stayed still, with the sun shining on it through the window pane; stayed still, as if the sun were a huge nail shooting through the pane and holding it down. It did not go up. It would not go up.

They would not come.

I knew it. Suddenly, just like that, snap, I knew they would not come; could not come. The shades would stay still. I knew they would not come. I lowered my hands, my eyes darting from shaded window to shaded window, around the yard, under the house, searching, for what? I did not know, and then there was the car. My eyes were glued to the car, and I started over to it, slowly at first, and then I ran and I stopped short and pressed my head up against the glass in the front door beside the steering wheel. The glass was hot on my nose and lips and forehead, and burned them, but I did not care, I pressed harder, as if by doing so I could push right through the glass, not breaking it, but melting through it. Then, I felt as though I *was* inside, in my favorite spot up front with Daddy, and in back were Mother Dear and John and our sisters; Daddy whistling and the trees going by and the farms and green, green, green, and other cars and Daddy starting to sing and all of us joining him singing "Choo-Choo Train to Town," even Jo Ann and Willie Mae, who had not learned the words yet, singing, singing, and ending laughing and feeling Daddy's hand on. my head.

"Jim." I turned from the window, and it was Aunt Mabel's hand on my head.

"Come on, son." She took my right hand and led me up the street as if I were a baby just starting to walk.

"What we going to do, Aunt Mabel?"

"You got to be brave, Jim. You the oldest. You got to look out for your brother and sisters."

I decided then that I would not let my brother and sisters see me cry, ever. I was twelve years old and the oldest, and I had to take care of them.

"When can we go back home, Aunt Mabel?"

"I guess we ought to move over to your house while we wait for the family to get here," Aunt Mabel said. "It's bigger than mine and your clothes there."

I looked up at Aunt Mabel. I had not expected her to move back with us. I wanted only we children to move back home.

When we got back to Aunt Mabel's house, I told John about the automobile accident and that Mother Dear and Daddy were dead. John was only eight, but he understood and he cried, and I understood just how he felt, so I left him alone.

The next day we moved back to our house. Aunt Mabel too. Every time one of our sisters would ask for Mother Dear and Daddy, we always said they were gone away. They were too young to understand about death.

Aunt Mabel told me that our Uncles and Aunts and Grandparents were coming. I didn't know any of them. I remembered Christmas presents from them and Mother Dear and Daddy talking about them, but I had never seen them.

"They're good folks," Aunt Mabel said, "and it won't make no difference which one you-all go to live with."

"But, Aunt Mabel. We going to stay home."

"You can't, son. You-all too young to stay here by yourself, and I can't take care of you."

"I can take care of us, Aunt Mabel. I'm the oldest. I can take care of us."

Aunt Mabel smiled. "Bet you could, too. But you-all need somebody to be a Mamma and a Papa to you. You-all got to go live with one of your Aunts and Uncles."

I knew right away that Aunt Mabel was right. I told John about it, and we started trying to guess where we would go. The family was scattered all over, mostly in big cities like New York, Philadelphia, and Boston. Our Grandfather on Daddy's side was in Texas. John and I couldn't decide what we liked best: Texas and horses or big cities and buildings. We talked about it every day while we waited for them to come, and now they were here.

I left the window and started to get dressed. John ran back into the room.

"Them won't wake up."

"They can sleep, then," I said. "Let's go see where the cars came from."

We got dressed and ran out to the yard and looked at the license plates. There were two from New York, two from Pennsylvania, and one from Massachusetts.

"None of them from Texas," I said.

"Which one you like best?" asked John.

"That one," I said, pointing to the one from Massachusetts. I liked it because it was the biggest one. The five of us could get in it without any trouble at all.

We examined each car carefully for an hour, and then Aunt Mabel called us and told us to come in the house.

"They all here," she said, "all that's coming, I guess. Now, you-all be good so they'll like you."

I followed Aunt Mabel into the living room. I could feel John right behind me, up close, and I could hear his breathing.

"Here the boys," Aunt Mabel announced, and walked across the room and sat down.

John and I stopped at the door. Our sisters were lined up, side by side, in the middle of the room, smiling. I had heard voices before we came into the room, but now, there was silence and all eyes were on us. They sat in a half circle in straight-back chairs, near the walls around the room. I looked at them. I stared at each face. Aunt Mabel and our sisters were the only smiling faces I saw. I didn't know about John, but right at that moment, I was scared. I wanted to turn and run away as fast as I could. I felt as if I had committed the worst crime and those faces hated me for it. Besides Aunt Mabel, there were five men and five women, all dressed in black. Each man had a black line above his upper lip. The two men who were fat had thick black lines, and the other three had thinner ones. I didn't like the lines. Daddy never wore one, and I always thought his face was cleaner and friendlier and happier than other men I had seen who wore them.

I noticed the features of these people right away. They were all like Mother Dear, Aunt Mabel, and our sisters, and they were pink rose. I knew they were Mother Dear's relatives. Daddy didn't have any brothers or sisters, and he used to tell John and me whenever we got into a fight with each other that we should be kind to each other because we were brothers and it was good to have a brother and that he wished he had had brothers and sisters. Mother Dear had plenty of brothers and sisters. She had three brothers, and I knew them right away as the three who weren't fat, and three sisters, Aunt Mabel, of course, and the two women who sat beside the fat men.

I stood there looking, staring at those faces that looked as if they had just taken straight castor oil. I looked at John, now standing at my right. He stood there with his mouth hanging open and his eyes straight ahead. I could tell he was scared, and as soon as I knew he was scared, I wasn't scared any more, and I wanted to tell him not to be scared, because I wasn't going to let anything happen to him. Just when I was about to tell him, Aunt Mabel broke the silence.

"Come on over here next to your sisters," she said.

We shuffled over to where our sisters were and stood there like slaves on auction.

"They good children," Aunt Mabel said. "No trouble at all."

The others still kept quiet, except for whispers among themselves.

"Say your names, boys," Aunt Mabel said.

"James," I said.

"John," said John.

"We call James, Jim," Aunt Mabel said, and smiled at me.

I looked at her. It was all right for her to call me Jim. Mother Dear and Daddy called me Jim. I looked back at those faces. I didn't want *them* to call me Jim.

"Well," Aunt Mabel said to them, "you-all going to tell the boys your names?"

They introduced themselves to us, not smiling, not changing those castor-oil expressions. Apparently they had already introduced themselves to our sisters.

"Mabel," one of the fat men said, "why don't you get these kids out of here so we can talk."

"Jim, you and the children go in the dining room," Aunt Mabel said, and when we were going, she added, "and close the door."

We went into the dining room and I closed the door. Our sisters sat down in the middle of the floor and played. John stood over them, watching, but when he saw me with my ear to the door, he came over and joined me. We faced each other with our heads pressed up against the door, and we listened. The only voice I could recognize was Aunt Mabel's.

"Carol and I have thought this thing over, and we can see our way clear to take the girls," one of the men said.

"Now, wait a minute, Sam," another woman said. "We thought we'd take *one* of the girls, at least."

Then, for a minute it sounded as if they were all trying to get a word in. They talked all at the same time, even yelled. It sounded as if everyone wanted a girl.

"Lord have mercy. You mean you going to split them up? You mean they won't be together?"

"Five kids? Frankly, we can't afford two, but we'd be willing to take the three girls."

There was another minute of all of them trying to speak at the same time, at the top of their voices, each one wanting a girl.

"Why don't you-all talk like people? I don't like to see

them split up, but I guess five is too many for anybody, specially when they not your own."

"Then you understand that they'll have to be separated? There's no other way, and since we already have a son, we thought we would take one of the girls."

"Well," Aunt Mabel said, "look like to me all you-all want a girl. I didn't hear nobody say nothing about the boys, yet."

There was silence. John and I pressed harder against the door. John's mouth was open, his bottom lip hanging, and he was staring at me hard. I could tell he was scared, and I must have looked scared to him, so I closed my own mouth and tried to swallow. There was nothing to swallow, and I had to open my mouth again and take a deep breath.

"Come to think of it, you-all didn't say one word to them boys," Aunt Mabel said. "Why don't you-all want boys?"

"We have a boy."

"We do, too."

"Girls are easier."

"Boys are impossible."

"Lord have mercy."

"Listen, Mabel, you don't understand the situation."

"Don't get on your high horse with me. Talk plain."

"All right, Mabel. The fact is, the boys are—well—they're too, well, too much like the father."

"What?"

"You heard me. I know that's why *we* don't want one, and it's probably why the others here don't want one, and it's no use avoiding it."

"Is that right? Is that why you-all don't want one, too?" Aunt Mabel asked.

There was silence.

"Lord have mercy. I never heard such a thing in all my life. Your own sister's children, too."

"You don't understand, Mabel."

"No, I don't. Lord knows I don't. What you-all doing up there? Passing? Huh? That what you doing? No. No. You couldn't be doing that. Even if you wanted to, you couldn't be doing that. You not that light that you can pass, none of you-all. Lord have mercy. They too black for you. Your own sister's children."

John looked down at his hands, at the back of his hands and then at me and down at our sisters and at his hands again.

"I never thought I'd live to see the day my own flesh and blood would talk like that, and all the trouble in the world. My own sisters and brothers," Aunt Mabel said.

"Mabel, you've been here in this town all your life. This town isn't the world. You don't know how it is."

John rubbed the back of his hand on his pants and looked at it again.

I kept listening.

"It's hard enough like it is without having these boys, having to always explain about them. You can see that, Mabel. Look at us, how light we are. We'd always have to explain to everyone they're our dead sister's boys, and people who we don't explain to will jump to all kinds of conclusions. Socially, we'd be out, too. No, Mabel. That's just the way it is, and we can't do a thing about it. I, for one, have certain standards I want to live up to, and having these boys won't help."

"I never thought it. I never thought it."

"That's the way it is, Mabel. Those boys will do none of us any good."

John went over to where our sisters played and stood over them, examining them.

Aunt Mabel said: "So that's how come you didn't want her to get married. That's how come you tried to get her away from here."

John kneeled down and touched each one of our sisters. He looked at them and at his hand, at them and at his hand, and then to me. Then, his eyes became shiny, and he started batting his eyes, and the sides of his face grew, his cheeks puffed way out, his mouth closed tight. He fought it all he could, and I knew it was useless; he would not succeed. I could feel the same thing happening to me, but I held it back and concentrated on him, watched his swelling face until it exploded, and thinking he might yell out, I rushed to him and got down on my knees and held him, held him close, just as Daddy would have, with my left arm around his back and my right hand behind his head, holding his head to my chest, and felt his body shaking like a balloon when you let out the air, and I listened to him groan like a whipped dog. I didn't say one word to him. I couldn't. I let him cry, and I held him and watched our sisters, and they suddenly realized he was crying, and they came to us and helped me hold him and tried to get him to tell why he cried, and when he would not tell, they asked me, and when I would not tell, they stood there holding both of us until John got control of himself. He sat back on his heels and sobbed, and the girls stepped back and watched him. I stood up and watched all of them. The girls stood there and watched him and waited, their faces alert, ready to run to him and help him. It was as if they knew, now, this was not a physical wound that made him cry, not a twisted arm, a stubbed toe, or a beating, and certainly not a cry that would make them laugh and yell "cry baby" at him. It was as if they knew it was a wound they had never had and that it was deeper than skin.

I heard the voices in the living room, louder now, and wilder, so I started back to my place at the door, but before I got there, John lost control again. We got to him at the same time and tried to hold him, but this time he pushed us away, fought us off, and got to his feet and ran into the living room. I got to my feet as fast as I could and ran after him into the living room. He was screaming now, and when I ran into the living room, I stopped short at what I saw. John had run in and jumped in the lap of the first man he came to, and he was there on his knees in the man's lap screaming and pounding the man's chest and face. The man pushed him off, and John fell to the floor on his back and got right up and jumped in the man's lap again, still screaming, and pounded the man's chest and face with both his little fists.

"John, John, John!" I yelled, and ran to him and pulled him out of the man's lap, just in time, too, because the man swung at him back-handed, but I had John down, and the man missed. John, still screaming, kicking, struggled with me, trying to get away from me so he could get back to the man.

"John, John!" I yelled, shaking him, trying to make him hear me. "John, John!" but I could see he wasn't listening to me even though he was looking straight at me as I stood in front of him holding both of his arms and shouting his name. He only screamed.

Suddenly, I started walking backwards from him, holding his arms still, pulling him along with me until we were in the center of the room, and then I smiled at him. "Come on, John, come on, John," I said, and laughed, laughed hard, looking into his eyes; I kept it up, laughed loud and harder still and felt my body shake from it. Then I saw John's face change, first a smile, then he broke into a laugh too. I stared into his eyes and we laughed. We laughed. We laughed. We laughed. We threw our heads back and we laughed. We held each other's hands and danced round and round and laughed. Our sisters came and joined our dance. We formed a circle, all of us laughing, laughing, and we danced round and round. We were the only people in the world. We danced round and round and laughed and laughed.

"Hey," I said, "Choo-Choo Train, Choo-Choo Train," and they joined me:

> "Choo-choo train, choo-choo train
> We going to take that choo-choo train
> Choo-choo train to town
> Choo-choo train
> Choo-choo train."

Round and round, "Choo-Choo Train" louder and louder I sang, "CHOO-CHOO TRAIN, CHOO-CHOO TRAIN, CHOO-CHOO TRAIN TO TEXAS" round and round "CHOO-CHOO TRAIN" until I realized what I had said, and I screamed happily and said it again and again until they caught on and said it too. We went faster and faster and said it louder and louder sounding like a choo-choo train: TEXAS, TEXAS, TEXAS, TEXAS, TEXAS....

FOR DISCUSSION

1. Why is Jim terrified when he walks into the living room and first confronts his relatives? Why do the relatives agree to take the girls to live with them but refuse to take Jim and John? What has caused this Black family to have such a callous attitude toward people with dark skin?

2. At the end of the story, the children are laughing, dancing, and singing. Are they all happy? What do you think will become of them?

Sterling A. Brown

b. 1901

Noted for his ballad-like narratives of racial protest, Sterling A. Brown has had a distinguished career as teacher, writer, and editor. An alumnus of Williams College, where he was elected to Phi Beta Kappa, he received his M.A. from Harvard. For many years a professor at Howard University, he has also been a visiting professor at New York University, Atlanta University, and Vassar. Brown has published a collection of his early poems and two volumes of literary criticism. He served as senior editor of The Negro Caravan, *an anthology of Black writing in America, and as Editor on Negro Affairs for the Federal Writers' Project.*

Remembering Nat Turner

(For R. C. L.)

We saw a bloody sunset over Courtland, once Jerusalem,
As we followed the trail that old Nat took
When he came out of Cross Keys down upon Jerusalem,
In his angry stab for freedom a hundred years ago.
The land was quiet, and the mist was rising,
Out of the woods and the Nottaway swamp,
Over Southampton the still night fell,
As we rode down to Cross Keys where the march began.

When we got to Cross Keys, they could tell us little of him,
The Negroes had only the faintest recollections:
  "I ain't been here so long, I come from up roun' New-
    some;
  Yassah, a town a few miles up de road,
  The old folks who coulda told you is all dead an' gone.
  I heard something, sometime; I doan jis remember what.
  'Pears lak I heard that name somewheres or other.
  So he fought to be free. Well. You doan say."

An old white woman recalled exactly
How Nat crept down the steps, axe in his hand,
After murdering a woman and child in bed,
"Right in this here house at the head of these stairs"
(In a house built long after Nat was dead).
She pointed to a brick store where Nat was captured,
(Nat was taken in the swamp, three miles away)
With his men around him, shooting from the windows
(She was thinking of Harper's Ferry and old John Brown).
She cackled as she told how they riddled Nat with bullets
(Nat was tried and hanged at Courtland, ten miles away).
She wanted to know why folks would come miles
Just to ask about an old nigger fool.
  "Ain't no slavery no more, things is going all right,
  Pervided thar's a good goober market this year.
  We had a signpost here with printing on it,
  But it rotted in the hole, and thar it lays,
  And the nigger tenants split the marker for kindling.
  Things is all right, naow, ain't no trouble with the niggers.
  Why they make this big to-do over Nat?"

As we drove from Cross Keys back to Courtland,
Along the way that Nat came down upon Jerusalem,
A watery moon was high in the cloud-filled heavens,
The same moon he dreaded a hundred years ago.
The tree they hanged Nat on is long gone to ashes,
The trees he dodged behind have rotted in the swamps.

The bus for Miami and the trucks boomed by,
And touring cars, their heavy tires snarling on the pave-
    ment.
Frogs piped in the marshes, and a hound bayed long,
And yellow lights glowed from the cabin windows.

As we came back the way that Nat led his army,
Down from Cross Keys, down to Jerusalem,
We wondered if his troubled spirit still roamed the Notta-
    way,
Or if it fled with the cock-crow at daylight,
Or lay at peace with the bones in Jerusalem,
Its restlessness stifled by Southampton clay.

We remembered the poster rotted through and falling,
The marker split for kindling a kitchen fire.

FOR DISCUSSION

How do the people whom the speaker meets remember Nat
Turner? What is the meaning of the last two lines?

Southern Cop

Let us forgive Ty Kendricks
The place was Darktown. He was young.
His nerves were jittery. The day was hot.
The Negro ran out of the alley.
And so Ty shot.

Let us understand Ty Kendricks
The Negro must have been dangerous,
Because he ran;
And here was a rookie with a chance
To prove himself man.

Let us condone Ty Kendricks
If we cannot decorate.
When he found what the Negro was running for,
It was all too late;
And all we can say for the Negro is
It was unfortunate.

Let us pity Ty Kendricks
He has been through enough,
Standing there, his big gun smoking,
Rabbit-scared, alone,
Having to hear the wenches wail
And the dying Negro moan.

FOR DISCUSSION

In the first line of each stanza, the speaker asks the reader to sympathize with Ty Kendricks, the Southern cop. Explain how the arguments offered in defense of Kendricks are ironic.

Robert Hayden

b. 1913

Recipient of the Grand Prize for Poetry for A Ballad of Remembrance *at the First World Festival of Negro Arts in Senegal, West Africa, in 1965, Robert Hayden has also been awarded several American prizes and fellowships for his poetry. He received the Hopwood Award from the University of Michigan in 1938 and 1942, a Rosenwald Fellowship in 1947, and a Ford Foundation grant in 1954. Black history and folklore are a subject of major interest for Hayden, and he often uses this material in his poems. A graduate of Wayne State University, Hayden is presently a professor of English at Fisk University and poetry editor of the Baha'i magazine* World Order.

Runagate Runagate

1

Runs falls rises stumbles on from darkness into darkness
and the darkness thicketed with shapes of terror
and the hunters pursuing and the hounds pursuing
and the night cold and the night long and the river
to cross and the jack-muh-lanterns beckoning beckoning
and blackness ahead and when shall I reach that some-
    where

RUNAGATE: fugitive; runaway.

morning and keep on going and never turn back and keep
    on going

    Runagate
          Runagate
               Runagate

Many thousands rise and go
many thousands crossing over

                        O mythic North
               O star-shaped yonder Bible city

Some go weeping and some rejoicing
some in coffins and some in carriages
some in silks and some in shackles

    Rise and go or fare you well

No more auction block for me
no more driver's lash for me

        If you see my Pompey, 30 yrs of age,
        new breeches, plain stockings, negro shoes;
        if you see my Anna, likely young mulatto
        branded E on the right cheek, R on the left,
        catch them if you can and notify subscriber.
        Catch them if you can, but it won't be easy.
        They'll dart underground when you try to catch them,
        plunge into quicksand, whirlpools, mazes,
        turn into scorpions when you try to catch them.

And before I'll be a slave
I'll be buried in my grave

        North star and bonanza gold
        I'm bound for the freedom, freedom-bound
        and oh Susyanna don't you cry for me

        Runagate

           Runagate

2

Rises from their anguish and their power,

Harriet Tubman,

woman of earth, whipscarred,
a summoning, a shining

Mean to be free

And this was the way of it, brethren brethren,
way we journeyed from Can't to Can.
Moon so bright and no place to hide,
the cry up and the patterollers[1] riding,
hound dogs belling in bladed air.
And fear starts a-murbling, Never make it,
we'll never make it. *Hush that now,*
and she's turned upon us, levelled pistol
glinting in the moonlight:
Dead folks can't jaybird-talk, she says;
you keep on going now or die, she says.

Wanted   Harriet Tubman   alias The General
alias Moses   Stealer of Slaves

In league with Garrison   Alcott   Emerson
Garrett   Douglass   Thoreau   John Brown

Armed and known to be Dangerous

Wanted   Reward   Dead or Alive

Tell me, Ezekiel, oh tell me do you see
mailed Jehovah coming to deliver me?

Hoot-owl calling in the ghosted air,
five times calling to the hants in the air.

[1] PATTEROLLERS: patrols appointed to capture runaway slaves.

Shadow of a face in the scary leaves,
shadow of a voice in the talking leaves:

> Come ride-a my train

> *Oh that train, ghost-story train*
> *through swamp and savanna movering movering,*
> *over trestles of dew, through caves of the wish,*
> *Midnight Special on a sabre track movering movering,*
> *first stop Mercy and the last Hallelujah.*

> Come ride-a my train

> Mean mean mean to be free.

FOR DISCUSSION

1. Describe the several voices that are speaking in this poem.

2. Why is it appropriate that Harriet Tubman is called "Moses"?

Frederick Douglass

When it is finally ours, this freedom, this liberty, this
    beautiful
and terrible thing, needful to man as air,
usable as earth; when it belongs at last to all,
when it is truly instinct, brain matter, diastole, systole,[1]
reflex action; when it is finally won; when it is more
than the gaudy mumbo jumbo of politicians:
this man, this Douglass, this former slave, this Negro
beaten to his knees, exiled, visioning a world
where none is lonely, none hunted, alien,
this man, superb in love and logic, this man
shall be remembered. Oh, not with statues' rhetoric,
not with legends and poems and wreaths of bronze alone,
but with the lives grown out of his life, the lives
fleshing his dream of the beautiful, needful thing.

[1] DIASTOLE (dī·ăs′tə·lē), SYSTOLE (sĭs′tə·lē): expansion, contraction (as in
   the pumping action of the heart).

FOR DISCUSSION

1. What do Hayden's images suggest about the nature of freedom?

2. Why does he repeatedly call Douglass a "man"?

Martin Luther King, Jr.

1929–1968

Awarded the Nobel Peace Prize for his efforts as a non-violent civil rights leader, Martin Luther King, Jr. was one of America's most outstanding Black spokesmen. Dr. King ended bus segregation in Montgomery, Alabama, through his carefully planned boycott of buses in that city. The organizer of the Southern Christian Leadership Conference, he staged mass demonstrations and carried his crusade for equality throughout the South.

In 1963 Dr. King led the famous March on Washington; the speech on the following pages was addressed to some 200,000 Freedom Marchers assembled there, and his dramatic efforts anticipated the Civil Rights Act passed a year later. He organized voter-registration drives in Alabama and led a march from Selma to Montgomery in 1965. In 1966 he focused his concern upon the slums of Chicago to call attention to de facto segregation in the North. In April, 1968, Dr. King journeyed to Memphis, Tennessee, to organize a demonstration in support of striking refuse workers. There he was shot to death by an assassin.

I Have a Dream

Five score years ago, a great American, in whose symbolic shadow we stand, signed the Emancipation Proclamation. This momentous decree came as a great beacon light of

137

hope to millions of Negro slaves who had been seared in the flames of withering injustice. It came as a joyous daybreak to end the long night of captivity.

But one hundred years later, we must face the tragic fact that the Negro is still not free. One hundred years later, the life of the Negro is still sadly crippled by the manacles of segregation and the chains of discrimination. One hundred years later, the Negro lives on a lonely island of poverty in the midst of a vast ocean of material prosperity. One hundred years later, the Negro is still languished in the corners of American society and finds himself an exile in his own land. So we have come here today to dramatize an appalling condition.

In a sense we have come to our nation's capital to cash a check. When the architects of our republic wrote the magnificent words of the Constitution and the Declaration of Independence, they were signing a promissory note to which every American was to fall heir. This note was a promise that all men would be guaranteed the unalienable rights of life, liberty, and the pursuit of happiness.

It is obvious today that America has defaulted on this promissory note insofar as her citizens of color are concerned. Instead of honoring this sacred obligation, America has given the Negro people a bad check, a check which has come back marked "insufficient funds." But we refuse to believe that the bank of justice is bankrupt. We refuse to believe that there are insufficient funds in the great vaults of opportunity of this nation. So we have come to cash this check—a check that will give us upon demand the riches of freedom and the security of justice. We have also come to this hallowed spot to remind America of the fierce urgency of *now*. This is no time to engage in the luxury of cooling off or to take the tranquilizing drug of gradualism. *Now* is the time to make real the promises of democracy. *Now* is the time to rise from the dark and desolate valley of segregation to the sunlit path of racial justice. *Now* is the time to open the doors of opportunity to all of God's children. *Now* is the time to lift our nation from the quicksands of racial injustice to the solid rock of brotherhood.

It would be fatal for the nation to overlook the urgency of the moment and to underestimate the determination of the Negro. This sweltering summer of the Negro's legitimate discontent will not pass until there is an invigorating autumn of freedom and equality. Nineteen sixty-three is not an end, but a beginning. Those who hope that the Negro needed to blow off steam and will now be content will have a rude awakening if the nation returns to business as usual. There will be neither rest nor tranquility in America until the Negro is granted his citizenship rights. The whirlwinds of revolt will continue to shake the foundations of our nation until the bright day of justice emerges.

But there is something that I must say to my people who stand on the warm threshold which leads into the palace of justice. In the process of gaining our rightful place we must not be guilty of wrongful deeds. Let us not seek to satisfy our thirst for freedom by drinking from the cup of bitterness and hatred. We must forever conduct our struggle on the high plane of dignity and discipline. We must not allow our creative protest to degenerate into physical violence. Again and again we must rise to the majestic heights of meeting physical force with soul force. The marvelous new militancy which has engulfed the Negro community must not lead us to a distrust of all white people, for many of our white brothers, as evidenced by their presence here today, have come to realize that their destiny is tied up with our destiny and their freedom is inextricably bound to our freedom. We cannot walk alone.

And as we walk, we must make the pledge that we shall march ahead. We cannot turn back. There are those who are asking the devotees of civil rights, "When will you be satisfied?" We can never be satisfied as long as the Negro is the victim of the unspeakable horrors of police brutality. We can never be satisfied as long as our bodies, heavy with the fatigue of travel, cannot gain lodging in the motels of the highways and the hotels of the cities. We cannot be satisfied as long as the Negro's basic mobility is from a smaller ghetto to a larger one. We can never be satisfied as long as a Negro in Mississippi cannot vote and a Negro in

New York believes he has nothing for which to vote. No, no, we are not satisfied, and we will not be satisfied until justice rolls down like waters and righteousness like a mighty stream.

I am not unmindful that some of you have come here out of great trials and tribulations. Some of you have come fresh from narrow jail cells. Some of you have come from areas where your quest for freedom left you battered by the storms of persecution and staggered by the winds of police brutality. You have been the veterans of creative suffering. Continue to work with the faith that unearned suffering is redemptive.

Go back to Mississippi, go back to Alabama, go back to South Carolina, go back to Georgia, go back to Louisiana, go back to the slums and the ghettos of our Northern cities, knowing that somehow this situation can and will be changed. Let us not wallow in the valley of despair.

I say to you today, my friends, that in spite of the difficulties and frustrations of the moment I still have a dream. It is a dream deeply rooted in the American dream.

I have a dream that one day this nation will rise up and live out the true meaning of its creed: "We hold these truths to be self-evident; that all men are created equal."

I have a dream that one day on the red hills of Georgia the sons of former slaves and the sons of former slave-owners will be able to sit down together at the table of brotherhood.

I have a dream that one day even the state of Mississippi, a desert state sweltering with the heat of injustice and oppression, will be transformed into an oasis of freedom and justice.

I have a dream that my four little children will one day live in a nation where they will not be judged by the color of their skin but by the content of their character.

I have a dream today.

I have a dream that one day the state of Alabama, whose governor's lips are presently dripping with the words of interposition and nullification, will be transformed into a situation where little black boys and black girls will be able to join hands with little white boys and white girls and walk together as sisters and brothers.

I have a dream today.

I have a dream that one day every valley shall be exalted, every hill and mountain shall be made low, the rough places will be made plain, and the crooked places will be made straight, and the glory of the Lord shall be revealed, and all flesh shall see it together.[1]

This is our hope. This is the faith with which I return to the South. With this faith we will be able to hew out of the mountain of despair a stone of hope. With this faith we will be able to transform the jangling discords of our nation into a beautiful symphony of brotherhood. With this faith we will be able to work together, to pray together, to struggle together, to go to jail together, to stand up for freedom together, knowing that we will be free one day.

This will be the day when all of God's children will be able to sing with new meaning

> "My country, 'tis of thee
> Sweet land of liberty,
>   Of thee I sing:
> Land where my fathers died,
> Land of the pilgrims' pride,
> From every mountain-side
>   Let freedom ring."

And if America is to be a great nation, this must become true. So let freedom ring from the prodigious hilltops of New Hampshire. Let freedom ring from the mighty mountains of New York. Let freedom ring from the heightening Alleghenies of Pennsylvania!

Let freedom ring from the snowcapped Rockies of Colorado!

Let freedom ring from the curvaceous peaks of California!

But not only that; let freedom ring from Stone Mountain of Georgia!

---

[1] EVERY VALLEY . . . TOGETHER: See Isaiah 40:4–5.

Let freedom ring from Lookout Mountain of Tennessee!
Let freedom ring from every hill and molehill of Mississippi. From every mountainside, let freedom ring.

When we let freedom ring, when we let it ring from every
village and every hamlet, from every state and every city,
we will be able to speed up that day when all of God's
children, black men and white men, Jews and Gentiles,
Protestants and Catholics, will be able to join hands and
sing in the words of the old Negro spiritual, "Free at last;
free at last! Thank God almighty, we are free at last!"

FOR DISCUSSION

1. Dr. King's famous speech is a very strong plea for nonviolence.
He even speaks of "creative suffering," and claims that "unearned
suffering is redemptive." Do you agree with his philosophy?

2. This speech, which Martin Luther King delivered in 1963, is
profoundly optimistic. On the basis of all that has happened since,
do you think his optimism was justified?

3. In the conclusion of his speech, Dr. King argues strongly for
integration. Do you think that full integration can be achieved?
Do you think that it is a desirable goal?

Eldridge Cleaver

b. 1935

Eldridge Cleaver, who describes himself as "a full-time revolutionary," is best known for his association with the Black Panther Party, an organization whose purpose is to protect Black people. Born in Little Rock, Arkansas, Cleaver grew up in the Black ghetto of Los Angeles. While serving a prison sentence, he began writing essays which were later published as the best seller Soul on Ice.

After his release from prison, Cleaver assumed the position of Minister of Information for the Black Panther Party. One of their most effective spokesmen, he began writing articles for Ramparts, Esquire, *and other magazines. In 1968 he was nominated for President by the Peace and Freedom Party. Earlier that year he was arrested for participating in a gun battle with police in California. Rather than return to prison, Cleaver fled the country.*

The White Race and Its Heroes

White people cannot, in the generality, be taken as models of how to live. Rather, the white man is himself in sore need of new standards, which will release him from his confusion and place him once again in fruitful communion with the depths of his own being.

James Baldwin
The Fire Next Time

143

Right from the go, let me make one thing absolutely clear: I am not now, nor have I ever been, a white man. Nor, I hasten to add, am I now a Black Muslim—although I used to be. But I *am* an Ofay[1] Watcher, a member of that unchartered, amorphous[2] league which has members on all continents and the islands of the seas. Ofay Watchers Anonymous, we might be called, because we exist concealed in the shadows wherever colored people have known oppression by whites, by white enslavers, colonizers, imperialists, and neo-colonialists.

Did it irritate you, compatriot, for me to string those epithets out like that? Tolerate me. My intention was not necessarily to sprinkle salt over anyone's wounds. I did it primarily to relieve a certain pressure on my brain. Do you cop that? If not, then we're in trouble, because we Ofay Watchers have a pronounced tendency to slip into that mood. If it is bothersome to you, it is quite a task for me because not too long ago it was my way of life to preach, as ardently as I could, that the white race is a race of devils, created by their maker to do evil, and make evil appear as good; that the white race is the natural, unchangeable enemy of the black man, who is the original man, owner, maker, cream of the planet Earth; that the white race was soon to be destroyed by Allah, and that the black man would then inherit the earth, which has always, in fact, been his.

I have, so to speak, washed my hands in the blood of the martyr, Malcolm X, whose retreat from the precipice of madness created new room for others to turn about in, and I am now caught up in that tiny space, attempting a maneuver of my own. Having renounced the teachings of Elijah Muhammad, I find that a rebirth does not follow automatically, of its own accord, that a void is left in one's vision, and this void seeks constantly to obliterate itself by pulling one back to one's former outlook. I have tried a tentative compromise by adopting a select vocabulary, so that now

---

[1] OFAY (ō'fā): slang for "white person."

[2] AMORPHOUS (ə·môr'fəs): having no specific form, organization, or character.

when I see the whites of *their* eyes, instead of saying "devil" or "beast" I say "imperialist" or "colonialist," and everyone seems to be happier.

In silence, we have spent our years watching the ofays, trying to understand them, on the principle that you have a better chance coping with the known than with the unknown. Some of us have been, and some still are, interested in learning whether it is *ultimately* possible to live in the same territory with people who seem so disagreeable to live with; still others want to get as far away from ofays as possible. What we share in common is the desire to break the ofays' power over us.

At times of fundamental social change, such as the era in which we live, it is easy to be deceived by the onrush of events, beguiled by the craving for social stability into mistaking transitory phenomena for enduring reality. The strength and permanence of "white backlash" in America is just such an illusion. However much this rear-guard action might seem to grow in strength, the initiative, and the future, rest with those whites and blacks who have liberated themselves from the master/slave syndrome.[3] And these are to be found mainly among the youth.

Over the past twelve years there has surfaced a political conflict between the generations that is deeper, even, than the struggle between the races. Its first dramatic manifestation was within the ranks of the Negro people, when college students in the South, fed up with Uncle Tom's hat-in-hand approach to revolution, threw off the yoke of the NAACP. When these students initiated the first sit-ins, their spirit spread like a raging fire across the nation, and the technique of nonviolent direct action, constantly refined and honed into a sharp cutting tool, swiftly matured. The older Negro "leaders," who are now all die-hard advocates of this tactic, scolded the students for sitting-in. The students rained down contempt upon their hoary heads. In the pre-sit-in days, these conservative leaders had always succeeded in putting down insurgent elements among the

[3] SYNDROME (sĭn'drōm): all the signs of a disease, disorder, or abnormality.

Negro people. (A measure of their power, prior to the students' rebellion, is shown by their success in isolating such great black men as the late W. E. B. DuBois and Paul Robeson, when these stalwarts, refusing to bite their tongues, lost favor with the U.S. Government by their unstinting efforts to link up the Negro revolution with national liberation movements around the world.)

The "Negro leaders," and the whites who depended upon them to control their people, were outraged by the impudence of the students. Calling for a moratorium on student initiative, they were greeted instead by an encore of sit-ins, and retired to their ivory towers to contemplate the new phenomenon. Others, less prudent because held on a tighter leash by the whites, had their careers brought to an abrupt end because they thought they could lead a black/white backlash against the students, only to find themselves in a kind of Bay of Pigs. Negro college presidents, who expelled students from all-Negro colleges in an attempt to quash the demonstrations, ended up losing their jobs; the victorious students would no longer allow them to preside over the campuses. The spontaneous protests on Southern campuses over the repressive measures of their college administrations were an earnest of the Free Speech upheaval which years later was to shake the UC campus at Berkeley. In countless ways, the rebellion of the black students served as catalyst for the brewing revolt of the whites.

What has suddenly happened is that the white race has lost its heroes. Worse, its heroes have been revealed as villains and its greatest heroes as the arch-villains. The new generations of whites, appalled by the sanguine and despicable record carved over the face of the globe by their race in the last five hundred years, are rejecting the panoply[4] of white heroes, whose heroism consisted in erecting the inglorious edifice of colonialism and imperialism; heroes whose careers rested on a system of foreign and domestic

[4] PANOPLY (păn'ə·plē): here, display of grandeur.

exploitation, rooted in the myth of white supremacy and the manifest destiny of the white race. The emerging shape of a new world order, and the requisites for survival in such a world, are fostering in young whites a new outlook. They recoil in shame from the spectacle of cowboys and pioneers —their heroic forefathers whose exploits filled earlier generations with pride—galloping across a movie screen shooting down Indians like Coke bottles. Even Winston Churchill, who is looked upon by older whites as perhaps the greatest hero of the twentieth century—even he, because of the system of which he was a creature and which he served, is an arch-villain in the eyes of the young white rebels.

At the close of World War Two, national liberation movements in the colonized world picked up new momentum and audacity, seeking to cash in on the democratic promises made by the Allies during the war. The Atlantic Charter, signed by President Roosevelt and Prime Minister Churchill in 1941, affirming "the right of all people to choose the form of government under which they may live," established the principle, although it took years of postwar struggle to give this piece of rhetoric even the appearance of reality. And just as world revolution has prompted the oppressed to re-evaluate their self-image in terms of the changing conditions, to slough off the servile attitudes inculcated by long years of subordination, the same dynamics of change have prompted the white people of the world to re-evaluate their self-image as well, to disabuse themselves of the Master Race psychology developed over centuries of imperial hegemony.[5]

It is among the white youth of the world that the greatest change is taking place. It is they who are experiencing the great psychic pain of waking into consciousness to find their inherited heroes turned by events into villains. Communication and understanding between the older and younger generations of whites has entered a crisis. The elders, who,

[5] HEGEMONY (hĭ·jĕm′ə·nē): dominant authority or influence.

in the tradition of privileged classes or races, genuinely do not understand the youth, trapped by old ways of thinking and blind to the future, have only just begun to be vexed— because the youth have only just begun to rebel. So thoroughgoing is the revolution in the psyches of white youth that the traditional tolerance which every older generation has found it necessary to display is quickly exhausted, leaving a gulf of fear, hostility, mutual misunderstanding, and contempt.

The rebellion of the oppressed peoples of the world, along with the Negro revolution in America, have opened the way to a new evaluation of history, a re-examination of the role played by the white race since the beginning of European expansion. The positive achievements are also there in the record, and future generations will applaud them. But there can be no applause now, not while the master still holds the whip in his hand! Not even the master's own children can find it possible to applaud him—he cannot even applaud himself! The negative rings too loudly. Slave-catchers, slaveowners, murderers, butchers, invaders, oppressors—the white heroes have acquired new names. The great white statesmen whom school children are taught to revere are revealed as the architects of systems of human exploitation and slavery. Religious leaders are exposed as condoners and justifiers of all these evil deeds. Schoolteachers and college professors are seen as a clique of brainwashers and whitewashers.

The white youth of today are coming to see, intuitively, that to escape the onus[6] of the history their fathers made they must face and admit the moral truth concerning the works of their fathers. That such venerated figures as George Washington and Thomas Jefferson owned hundreds of black slaves, that all of the Presidents up to Lincoln presided over a slave state, and that every President since Lincoln connived politically and cynically with the issues affecting the human rights and general welfare of the broad

---

[6] ONUS (ō'nəs): burden; blame.

masses of the American people—these facts weigh heavily upon the hearts of these young people.

The elders do not like to give these youngsters credit for being able to understand what is going on and what has gone on. When speaking of juvenile delinquency, or the rebellious attitude of today's youth, the elders employ a glib rhetoric. They speak of the "alienation of youth," the desire of the young to be independent, the problems of "the father image" and "the mother image" and their effect upon growing children who lack sound models upon which to pattern themselves. But they consider it bad form to connect the problems of the youth with the central event of our era—the national liberation movements abroad and the Negro revolution at home. The foundations of authority have been blasted to bits in America because the whole society has been indicted, tried, and convicted of injustice. To the youth, the elders are Ugly Americans; to the elders, the youth have gone mad.

The rebellion of the white youth has gone through four broadly discernible stages. First there was an initial recoiling away, a rejection of the conformity which America expected, and had always received, sooner or later, from its youth. The disaffected youth were refusing to participate in the system, having discovered that America, far from helping the underdog, was up to its ears in the mud trying to hold the dog down. Because of the publicity and self-advertisements of the more vocal rebels, this period has come to be known as the beatnik era, although not all of the youth affected by these changes thought of themselves as beatniks. The howl of the beatniks and their scathing, outraged denunciation of the system—characterized by Ginsberg as Moloch, a bloodthirsty Semitic deity to which the ancient tribes sacrificed their firstborn children—was a serious, irrevocable declaration of war. It is revealing that the elders looked upon the beatniks as mere obscene misfits who were too lazy to take baths and too stingy to buy a haircut. The elders had eyes but couldn't see, ears but couldn't hear—not even when the message came through as clearly as in this remarkable passage from Jack Kerouac's *On the Road:*

> "At lilac evening I walked with every muscle aching among the lights of 27th and Welton in the Denver colored section, wishing I were a Negro, feeling that the best the white world had offered was not enough ecstasy for me, not enough life, joy, kicks, darkness, music, not enough night. I wished I were a Denver Mexican, or even a poor overworked Jap, anything but what I so drearily was, a 'white man' disillusioned. All my life I'd had white ambitions. . . . I passed the dark porches of Mexican and Negro homes; soft voices were there; occasionally the dusky knee of some mysterious sensuous gal; the dark faces of the men behind rose arbors. Little children sat like sages in ancient rocking chairs."

The second stage arrived when these young people, having decided emphatically that the world, and particularly the U.S.A., was unacceptable to them in its present form, began an active search for roles they could play in changing the society. If many of these young people were content to lay up in their cool beat pads, smoking pot and listening to jazz in a perpetual orgy of esoteric bliss, there were others, less crushed by the system, who recognized the need for positive action. Moloch could not ask for anything more than to have its disaffected victims withdraw into safe, passive, apolitical little nonparticipatory islands, in an economy less and less able to provide jobs for the growing pool of unemployed. If all the unemployed had followed the lead of the beatniks, Moloch would gladly have legalized the use of euphoric drugs and marijuana, passed out free jazz albums and sleeping bags, to all those willing to sign affidavits promising to remain "beat." The non-beat disenchanted white youth were attracted magnetically to the Negro revolution, which had begun to take on a mass, insurrectionary tone. But they had difficulty understanding their relationship to the Negro, and what role "whites" could play in a "Negro revolution." For the time being they watched the Negro activists from afar.

The third stage, which is rapidly drawing to a close, emerged when white youth started joining Negro demonstrations in large numbers. The presence of whites among the demonstrators emboldened the Negro leaders and allowed them to use tactics they never would have been able to employ with all-black troops. The racist conscience of America is such that murder does not register as murder, really, unless the victim is white. And it was only when the newspapers and magazines started carrying pictures and stories of white demonstrators being beaten and maimed by mobs and police that the public began to protest. Negroes have become so used to this double standard that they, too, react differently to the death of a white. When white freedom riders were brutalized along with blacks, a sigh of relief went up from the black masses, because the blacks knew that white blood is the coin of freedom in a land where for four hundred years black blood has been shed unremarked and with impunity. America has never truly been outraged by the murder of a black man, woman, or child. White politicians may, if Negroes are aroused by a particular murder, say with their lips what they know with their minds they should feel with their hearts—but don't.

It is a measure of what the Negro feels that when the two white and one black civil rights workers were murdered in Mississippi in 1964, the event was welcomed by Negroes on a level of understanding beyond and deeper than the grief they felt for the victims and their families. This welcoming of violence and death to whites can almost be heard —indeed it can be heard—in the inevitable words, oft repeated by Negroes, that those whites, and blacks, do not die in vain. So it was with Mrs. Viola Liuzzo.[7] And much of the anger which Negroes felt toward Martin Luther King

[7] MRS. VIOLA LIUZZO: white civil rights worker shot to death near Selma, Alabama, at the time of the Selma-Montgomery march in 1965.

during the Battle of Selma stemmed from the fact that he denied history a great moment, never to be recaptured, when he turned tail on the Edmund Pettus Bridge and refused to all those whites behind him what they had traveled thousands of miles to receive. If the police had turned them back by force, all those nuns, priests, rabbis, preachers, and distinguished ladies and gentlemen old and young—as they had done the Negroes a week earlier—the violence and brutality of the system would have been ruthlessly exposed. Or if, seeing King determined to lead them on to Montgomery, the troopers had stepped aside to avoid precisely the confrontation that Washington would not have tolerated, it would have signaled the capitulation of the militant white South. As it turned out, the March on Montgomery was a show of somewhat dim luster, stage-managed by the Establishment. But by this time the young whites were already active participants in the Negro revolution. In fact they had begun to transform it into something broader, with the potential of encompassing the whole of America in a radical reordering of society.

The fourth stage, now in its infancy, sees these white youth taking the initiative, using techniques learned in the Negro struggle to attack problems in the general society. The classic example of this new energy in action was the student battle on the UC campus at Berkeley, California— the Free Speech Movement. Leading the revolt were veterans of the civil rights movement, some of whom spent time on the firing line in the wilderness of Mississippi/Alabama. Flowing from the same momentum were student demonstrations against U.S. interference in the internal affairs of Vietnam, Cuba, the Dominican Republic, and the Congo and U.S. aid to apartheid in South Africa. The students even aroused the intellectual community to actions and positions unthinkable a few years ago: witness the teach-ins. But their revolt is deeper than single-issue protest. The characteristics of the white rebels which most alarm their elders—the long hair, the new dances, their love for Negro music, their use of marijuana, their mystical attitude toward sex—are all tools of their rebellion. They have turned these tools against the totalitarian fabric of American society—and they mean to change it.

From the beginning, America has been a schizophrenic nation. Its two conflicting images of itself were never reconciled, because never before has the survival of its most cherished myths made a reconciliation mandatory. Once before, during the bitter struggle between North and South climaxed by the Civil War, the two images of America came into conflict, although whites North and South scarcely understood it. The image of America held by its most alienated citizens was advanced neither by the North nor by the South; it was perhaps best expressed by Frederick Douglass, who was born into slavery in 1817, escaped to the North, and became the greatest leader-spokesman for the blacks of his era. In words that can still, years later, arouse an audience of black Americans, Frederick Douglass delivered, in 1852, a scorching indictment in his Fourth of July oration in Rochester:

> "What to the American slave is your Fourth of July? I answer: a day that reveals to him, more than all other days in the year, the gross injustice and cruelty to which he is the constant victim. To him your celebration is a sham; your boasted liberty, an unholy license; your national greatness, swelling vanity; your sounds of rejoicing are empty and heartless; your denunciation of tyrants, brass-fronted impudence; your shouts of liberty and equality, hollow mockery; your prayers and hymns, your sermons and thanksgivings, with all your religious parade and solemnity, are, to him, more bombast, fraud, deception, impiety and hypocrisy—a thin veil to cover up crimes which would disgrace a nation of savages. . . ."

> "You boast of your love of liberty, your superior civilization, and your pure Christianity, while the whole political power of the nation (as em-

bodied in the two great political parties) is solemnly pledged to support and perpetuate the
enslavement of three millions of your country-
men. You hurl your anathemas[8] at the crown-
headed tyrants of Russia and Austria and pride
yourselves on your democratic institutions, while
you yourselves consent to be the mere *tools* and
bodyguards of the tyrants of Virginia and Carolina."

"You invite to your shores fugitives of oppression from abroad, honor them with banquets,
greet them with ovations, cheer them, toast them,
salute them, protect them, and pour out your
money to them like water; but the fugitive from
your own land you advertise, hunt, arrest, shoot,
and kill. You glory in your refinement and your
universal education; yet you maintain a system
as barbarous and dreadful as ever stained the
character of a nation—a system begun in avarice,
supported in pride, and perpetuated in cruelty."

"You shed tears over fallen Hungary, and make
the sad story of her wrongs the theme of your
poets, statesmen, and orators, till your gallant
sons are ready to fly to arms to vindicate her
cause against the oppressor; but, in regard to the
ten thousand wrongs of the American slave, you
would enforce the strictest silence, and would
hail him as an enemy of the nation who dares to
make these wrongs the subject of public dis-
course!"

This most alienated view of America was preached by the
Abolitionists, and by Harriet Beecher Stowe in her *Uncle
Tom's Cabin*. But such a view of America was too dis-
tasteful to receive wide attention, and serious debate about

[8] ANATHEMAS (ə·năth'ə·məz): denunciations; curses.

America's image and her reality was engaged in only on the fringes of society. Even when confronted with overwhelming evidence to the contrary, most white Americans have found it possible, after steadying their rattled nerves, to settle comfortably back into their vaunted belief that America is dedicated to the proposition that all men are created equal and endowed by their Creator with certain inalienable rights—life, liberty, and the pursuit of happiness. With the Constitution for a rudder and the Declaration of Independence as its guiding star, the ship of state is sailing always toward a brighter vision of freedom and justice for all.

Because there is no common ground between these two contradictory images of America, they had to be kept apart. But the moment the blacks were let into the white world— let out of the voiceless and faceless cages of their ghettos, singing, walking, talking, dancing, writing, and orating *their* image of America and of Americans—the white world was suddenly challenged to match its practice to its preachments. And this is why those whites who abandon the *white* image of America and adopt the *black* are greeted with such unmitigated hostility by their elders.

For all these years whites have been taught to believe in the myth they preached, while Negroes have had to face the bitter reality of what America practiced. But without the lies and distortions, white Americans would not have been able to do the things they have done. When whites are forced to look honestly upon the objective proof of their deeds, the cement of mendacity[9] holding white society together swiftly disintegrates. On the other hand, the core of the black world's vision remains intact, and in fact begins to expand and spread into the psychological territory vacated by the nonviable white lies, i.e., into the minds of young whites. It is remarkable how the system worked for so many years, how the majority of whites remained effectively unaware of any contradiction between their view of the world and that world itself. The mechanism by which

[9] MENDACITY (měn·dăs′ə·tē): state or quality of being inclined to practice deception.

this was rendered possible requires examination at this point.

Let us recall that the white man, in order to justify slavery and, later on, to justify segregation, elaborated a complex, all-pervasive myth which at one time classified the black man as a subhuman beast of burden. The myth was progressively modified, gradually elevating the blacks on the scale of evolution, following their slowly changing status, until the plateau of separate-but-equal was reached at the close of the nineteenth century. During slavery, the black was seen as a mindless Supermasculine Menial. Forced to do the backbreaking work, he was conceived in terms of his ability to do such work—"field niggers," etc. The white man administered the plantation, doing all the thinking, exercising omnipotent power over the slaves. He had little difficulty dissociating himself from the black slaves, and he could not conceive of their positions being reversed or even reversible.

Blacks and whites being conceived as mutually exclusive types, those attributes imputed to the blacks could not also be imputed to the whites—at least not in equal degree—without blurring the line separating the races. These images were based upon the social function of the two races, the work they performed. The ideal white man was one who knew how to use his head, who knew how to manage and control things and get things done. Those whites who were not in a position to perform these functions nevertheless aspired to them. The ideal black man was one who did exactly as he was told, and did it efficiently and cheerfully. "Slaves," said Frederick Douglass, "are generally expected to sing as well as to work." As the black man's position and function became more varied, the images of white and black, having become stereotypes, lagged behind.

The separate-but-equal doctrine was promulgated by the Supreme Court in 1896. It had the same purpose domestically as the Open Door Policy toward China in the international arena: to stabilize a situation and subordinate a nonwhite population so that racist exploiters could manipulate those people according to their own selfish interests. These doctrines were foisted off as *the epitome of enlightened justice, the highest expression of morality.* Sanctified by religion, justified by philosophy, and legalized by the Supreme Court, separate-but-equal was enforced by day by agencies of the law, and by the KKK & Co. under cover of night. Booker T. Washington, the Martin Luther King of his day, accepted separate-but-equal in the name of all Negroes. W. E. B. DuBois denounced it.

Separate-but-equal marked the last stage of the white man's flight into cultural neurosis, and the beginning of the black man's frantic striving to assert his humanity and equalize his position with the white. Blacks ventured into all fields of endeavor to which they could gain entrance. Their goal was to present in all fields a performance that would equal or surpass that of the whites. It was long axiomatic among blacks that a black had to be twice as competent as a white in any field in order to win grudging recognition from the whites. This produced a pathological motivation in blacks to equal or surpass the whites, and a pathological motivation in the whites to maintain a distance from the blacks. This is the rack on which black and white Americans receive their delicious torture! At first there was the color bar, flatly denying the blacks entrance to certain spheres of activity. When this no longer worked, and blacks invaded sector after sector of American life and economy, the whites evolved other methods of keeping their distance. The illusion of the Negro's inferior nature had to be maintained.

One device evolved by the whites was to tab whatever the blacks did with the prefix "Negro." We had *Negro* literature, *Negro* athletes, *Negro* music, *Negro* doctors, *Negro* politicians, *Negro* workers. The malignant ingeniousness of this device is that although it accurately describes an objective biological fact—or, at least, a sociological fact in America—it concealed the paramount psychological fact: that to the white mind, prefixing anything with "Negro" automatically consigned it to an inferior category. A well-known example of the white necessity to deny due credit to blacks is in the realm of music. White musicians were famous for going to Harlem and other Negro cultural centers literally to steal the black man's music, carrying it back across the color line into the Great White World and passing off the watered-down loot as their own original creations. Blacks, meanwhile, were ridiculed as *Negro* musicians playing inferior coon music.

The Negro revolution at home and national liberation movements abroad have unceremoniously shattered the world of fantasy in which the whites have been living. It is painful that many do not yet see that their fantasy world has been rendered uninhabitable in the last half of the twentieth century. But it is away from this world that the white youth of today are turning. The "paper tiger" hero James Bond, offering the whites a triumphant image of themselves, is saying what many whites want desperately to hear reaffirmed: *I am still the White Man, lord of the land, licensed to kill, and the world is still an empire at my feet.* James Bond feeds on that secret little anxiety, the psychological white backlash, felt in some degree by most whites alive. It is exasperating to see little brown men and little yellow men from the mysterious Orient, and the opaque black men of Africa (to say nothing of these impudent American Negroes!) who come to the UN and talk smart to us, who are scurrying all over *our* globe in their strange modes of dress—much as if they were new, unpleasant arrivals from another planet. Many whites believe in their ulcers that it is only a matter of time before the Marines get the signal to round up these truants and put them back securely in their cages. But it is away from this fantasy world that the white youth of today are turning.

In the world revolution now under way, the initiative rests with people of color. That growing numbers of white youth are repudiating their heritage of blood and taking people of color as their heroes and models is a tribute not only to their insight but to the resilience of the human spirit.

For today the heroes of the initiative are people not usually thought of as white: Fidel Castro, Che Guevara, Kwame Nkrumah, Mao Tse-tung, Gamal Abdel Nasser, Robert F. Williams, Malcolm X, Ben Bella, John Lewis, Martin Luther King, Jr., Robert Parris Moses, Ho Chi Minh, Stokely Carmichael, W. E. B. DuBois, James Forman, Chou En-lai.

The white youth of today have begun to react to the fact that the "American Way of Life" is a fossil of history. What do they care if their old baldheaded and crew-cut elders don't dig their caveman mops? They couldn't care less about the old honkies who don't like their new dances: Frug, Monkey, Jerk, Swim, Watusi. All they know is that it feels good to swing to way-out body rhythms instead of dragging across the dance floor like zombies to the dead beat of mind-smothered Mickey Mouse music. Is it any wonder that the youth have lost all respect for their elders, for law and order, when for as long as they can remember all they've witnessed is a monumental bickering over the Negro's place in American society and the right of people around the world to be left alone by outside powers? They have witnessed the law, both domestic and international, being spat upon by those who do not like its terms. Is it any wonder, then, that they feel justified, by sitting-in and freedom riding, in breaking laws made by lawless men? Old funny-styled, zipper-mouthed political night riders know nothing but to haul out an investigating committee *to look into the disturbance* to find the cause of the unrest among the youth. Look into a mirror! The cause is you, Mr. and Mrs. Yesterday, you with your forked tongues.

A young white today cannot help but recoil from the base deeds of his people. On every side, on every continent, he sees racial arrogance, savage brutality toward the conquered and subjugated people, genocide; he sees the human cargo of the slave trade; he sees the systematic extermination of American Indians; he sees the civilized nations of Europe fighting in imperial depravity over the lands of other people—and over possession of the very people themselves. There seems to be no end to the ghastly deeds of which his people are guilty. *GUILTY*. The slaughter of the Jews by the Germans, the dropping of atomic bombs on the Japanese people—these deeds weigh heavily upon the prostrate souls and tumultuous consciences of the white youth. The white heroes, their hands dripping with blood, are dead.

The young whites know that the colored people of the world, Afro-Americans included, do not seek revenge for their suffering. They seek the same things the white rebel wants: an end to war and exploitation. Black and white, the young rebels are free people, free in a way that Americans have never been before in the history of their country. And they are outraged.

There is in America today a generation of white youth that is truly worthy of a black man's respect, and this is a rare event in the foul annals of American history. From the beginning of the contact between blacks and whites, there has been very little reason for a black man to respect a white, with such exceptions as John Brown and others lesser known. But respect commands itself, and it can neither be given nor withheld when it is due. If a man like Malcolm X could change and repudiate racism, if I myself and other former Muslims can change, if young whites can change, then there is hope for America. It was certainly strange to find myself, while steeped in the doctrine that all whites were devils by nature, commanded by the heart to applaud and acknowledge respect for these young whites —despite the fact that they are descendants of the masters and I the descendant of slaves. The sins of the fathers are visited upon the heads of the children—but only if the children continue in the evil deeds of the fathers.

FOR DISCUSSION

1. Cleaver says that young people today have new and different heroes from those of their parents. Who are your heroes? Are they different from those of your parents? If so, how do they differ?

2. Cleaver says: "The characteristics of the white rebels which most alarm their elders—the long hair, the new dances, their love for Negro music, their use of marijuana, their mystical attitude toward sex—are all tools of their rebellion." Explain what Cleaver means by tools. Do you think the tools he mentions are effective?

3. Cleaver describes Americans as "schizophrenic," as people who preach justice and practice intolerance. How does this sort of schizophrenia affect individuals as well as the whole nation?

4. Cleaver says that the "conflict between the generations . . . is deeper, even, than the struggle between the races." Do you agree? In the last paragraph Cleaver expresses hope that both conflicts can be favorably resolved. Does your experience cause you to be equally optimistic?

Samuel Allen

b. 1917

Samuel Allen is a lawyer who has turned to letters and is now teaching African and Afro-American literature at Boston University. Allen was born in Columbus, Ohio, and studied creative writing under James Weldon Johnson at Fisk University. He also studied at Harvard Law School, the Sorbonne in Paris, and the New School for Social Research. His talent as a poet was recognized in Paris by Richard Wright, who encouraged Allen and published some of his poems in Présence Africaine, *the cultural journal of the African world. Since that time, Allen's verse has been frequently anthologized, sometimes under the pen name Paul Vesey. He has written a number of essays and is presently editing an anthology of African poetry to be published by Thomas Y. Crowell Company.*

A Moment Please

> *When I gaze at the sun*
> I walked to the subway booth
> for change for a dime.
> *and know that this great earth*
> Two adolescent girls stood there
> alive with eagerness to know
> *is but a fragment from it thrown*

162

all in their new found world
there was for them to know
in heat and flame a billion years ago,
   they looked at me and brightly asked
   "Are you Arabian?"
that then this world was lifeless
   I smiled and cautiously
   —for one grows cautious—
   shook my head.
as, a billion hence,
   "Egyptian?"
it shall again be,
   Again I smiled and shook my head
   and walked away.
what moment is it that I am betrayed,
   I've gone but seven paces now
oppressed, cast down,
   and from behind comes swift the sneer
or warm with love or triumph?
   "Or Nigger?"

   A moment, please
What is it that to fury I am roused?
   for still it takes a moment
What meaning for me
   and now
in this homeless clan
   I'll turn
the dupe of space
   and smile
the toy of time?
   and nod my head.

FOR DISCUSSION

What is the incident the poet is describing in the lines in regular type? What is he saying in the lines in italics? Why is the poem entitled "A Moment Please"?

Imamu Amiri Baraka

b. 1934

Imamu Amiri Baraka (LeRoi Jones) has written, "Any man black or white has something to say, but a black man these days will seem to have something more profound to say." The message he conveys in his writing comes across to his audience with raw power and explosive violence. Dutchman, *his first professionally produced play, won him the 1964 off-Broadway Obie Award, and production of* The Slave, The Toilet, The Eighth Ditch, *and* The Baptism *have also called attention to his forceful artistic talent. But Baraka views himself primarily as a poet.* Preface to a Twenty Volume Suicide Note, *published in 1961, typifies his difficult poetic form. Known for his involvement in social and political affairs, he has written numerous social essays published in* Negro Digest *and* Evergreen Review.

Preface to a Twenty Volume Suicide Note

For Kellie Jones, Born 16 May 1959

Lately, I've become accustomed to the way
The ground opens up and envelops me
Each time I go out to walk the dog.

164

Or the broad-edged silly music the wind
Makes when I run for a bus . . .

Things have come to that.

And now, each night I count the stars,
And each night I get the same number.
And when they will not come to be counted,
I count the holes they leave.

Nobody sings anymore.

And then last night, I tiptoed up
To my daughter's room and heard her
Talking to someone, and when I opened
The door, there was no one there . . .
Only she on her knees, peeking into

Her own clasped hands.

FOR DISCUSSION

1. Describe the speaker of this poem. How does the line "Nobody sings anymore" summarize his attitude toward his life?

2. What is the speaker's daughter doing in the last stanza? Is the ending of the poem hopeful?